PSYOP

PSYOP

PSYCHOLOGICAL OPERATIONS MANUAL

THE U.S. DEPARTMENT OF THE ARMY

Skyhorse Publishing

Skyhorse Publishing books may be purchased in bulk at special discounts for sales promotion, corporate gifts, fund-raising, or educational purposes. Special editions can also be created to specifications. For details, contact the Special Sales Department, Skyhorse Publishing, 307 Fifth Avenue, 4th Floor, New York, NY 10016 or info@skyhorsepublishing.com.

Visit our website at www.skyhorsepublishing.com.

10 9 8 7 6 5 4 3 2 1

Library of Congress Cataloging-in-Publication Data is available on file.

Cover design by Kai Texel

Print ISBN: 978-1-5107-8771-1
Ebook ISBN: 978-1-5107-8772-8

Printed in the United States of America

CONTENTS

PREFACE

Field Manual (FM) 3-05.30 is the keystone publication for Psychological Operations (PSYOP) principles. It is directly linked to, and must be used with, the doctrinal principles found in FM 3-0, *Operations*; FM 3-13, *Information Operations: Doctrine, Tactics, Techniques, and Procedures*; FM 100-25, *Doctrine for Army Special Operations Forces*; and Joint Publication (JP) 3-53, *Doctrine for Joint Psychological Operations*. It illustrates how PSYOP forces function for the supported commander and impact on the operating environment. This manual explains PSYOP fundamentals, unit functions and missions, command and control (C2) capabilities, and task organization. It also describes the PSYOP planning procedures, the employment of forces, and the intelligence and logistics support operations for PSYOP. FM 3-05.30 provides the authoritative foundation for PSYOP doctrine, training, leader development, organizational design, materiel acquisition, and Soldier systems. It is not intended exclusively for the PSYOP community; rather, it is intended to a large degree for supported commanders, regardless of Service, at all levels and their operations officers who will be supported by, and supervise, PSYOP personnel. PSYOP commanders and trainers at all levels should use this manual with Army mission training plans to develop and conduct their training.

This manual is unclassified to ensure its Armywide dissemination and the integration of PSYOP into the Army's system. As the proponent for PSYOP doctrine and training, the United States Army John F. Kennedy Special Warfare Center and School (USAJFKSWCS) published an additional FM, which is FM 3-05.301, *Psychological Operations Tactics, Techniques, and Procedures*, to disseminate the specific tactics, techniques, and procedures necessary to plan and conduct PSYOP. It will also publish FM 3-05.302, *Tactical Psychological Operations Tactics, Techniques, and*

Procedures, Army Training and Evaluation Programs (ARTEPs) for specific unit-level training, and the Soldier training publication (STP) for the 37F military occupational specialty (MOS). The provisions of FM 3-05.30 are subject to the international agreements listed in the Bibliography. There are numerous terms, acronyms, and abbreviations found within this manual. Users should refer to the Glossary for their meaning or definition.

The proponent of this publication is USAJFKSWCS. Submit comments and recommended changes to Commander, USAJFKSWCS, ATTN: AOJK-DTD-PO, Fort Bragg, NC 28310-5000.

Unless this publication states otherwise, masculine nouns and pronouns do not refer exclusively to men.

Chapter 1

INTRODUCTION TO PSYCHOLOGICAL OPERATIONS

The supported commander must integrate and synchronize many activities including PSYOP into a cohesive and successful military operation. The decisions made, from personnel through intelligence operations and logistics, can be staggering, even in a single-Service action. The task becomes more complex when the supported commander—as is so often the case—assumes responsibility for a joint or combined force. The supported commander will likely make one or more key decisions in a particular area that will have a psychological effect. As a result, he frames, and thereby determines, the actions of subordinate commanders and staffs with PSYOP in mind as they prosecute a campaign.

This chapter outlines critical decision points in the conduct of PSYOP at which supported commanders can influence the PSYOP effort. It also notes that in the modern media environment, PSYOP are among the sensitive areas requiring daily attention from the supported commander. Commanders plan PSYOP to convey selected information and indicators to foreign audiences to influence their emotions, motives, objective reasoning and, ultimately, the behavior of foreign governments, organizations, groups, and individuals.

> *Psychological operations...have proven to be indispensable...it allowed us to apply a type of power without necessarily having to shoot bullets.*
>
> Colonel Andy Birdy, Commander,
> 1st Brigade Combat Team, 10th Mountain Division,
> during Operation UPHOLD DEMOCRACY in Haiti

OVERVIEW

1-1. PSYOP are a vital part of the broad range of United States (U.S.) diplomatic, informational, military, and economic (DIME) activities. The employment of any element of national power, particularly the military element, has always had a psychological dimension. Foreign perceptions of U.S. military capabilities are fundamental to strategic deterrence. The effectiveness of deterrence hinges on U.S. ability to influence the perceptions of others. The purpose of PSYOP is to induce or reinforce foreign attitudes and behavior favorable to U.S. national objectives. PSYOP are characteristically delivered as information for effect, used during peacetime and conflict, to inform and influence. When properly employed, PSYOP can save lives of friendly and adversary forces by reducing the adversaries' will to fight. By lowering adversary morale and reducing their efficiency, PSYOP can also discourage aggressive actions and create dissidence and disaffection within their ranks, ultimately inducing surrender. PSYOP provide a commander the means to employ a nonlethal capability across the range of military operations from peace through conflict to war and during postconflict operations.

1-2. PSYOP forces primarily conduct operations at the operational and tactical levels of war, and during military operations other than war (MOOTW). PSYOP forces also support strategic operations. At the operational level, they support combatant commanders and commanders, joint task forces (CJTFs). At the tactical level, PSYOP forces support conventional forces and special operations forces (SOF). PSYOP units can conduct strategic activities in support of the President and/or Secretary of Defense (SecDef) and the Chairman of the Joint Chiefs of Staff (CJCS), when directed. PSYOP are inherently joint, frequently combined, and must be integrated and synchronized at all echelons to achieve their full force-multiplier potential.

1-3. Supported commanders establish a Psychological Operations task force (POTF)/Psychological Operations support element (PSE) that is normally under the operational control of a joint task force (JTF). The POTF will develop a PSYOP support plan derived from the CJTF campaign plan. This plan provides the guidance and direction for conducting PSYOP.

1-4. Unit commanders integrate aspects of planned PSYOP in several ways. They further the PSYOP objectives of the President and/or SecDef, geographic combatant commander, and JTF by conducting Psychological Operations actions (PSYACTs) and PSYOP enabling actions that directly support these objectives. Unit commanders also direct the employment of and protect attached PSYOP forces, which further maximize the effectiveness of the maneuver and PSYOP objective.

MISSION OF PSYOP

1-5. The mission of PSYOP is to influence the behavior of foreign target audiences (TAs) to support U.S. national objectives. PSYOP accomplish this by conveying selected information and/or advising on actions that influence the emotions, motives, objective reasoning, and ultimately the behavior of foreign audiences. Behavioral change is at the root of the PSYOP mission. Although concerned with the mental processes of the TA, it is the observable modification of TA behavior that determines the mission success of PSYOP. It is this link between influence and behavior that distinguishes PSYOP from other capabilities and activities of information operations (IO) and sets it apart as a unique core capability.

1-6. As a core capability of IO, PSYOP are considered primarily to be shaping operations that create and preserve opportunities for decisive operations. PSYOP help shape both the physical and informational dimensions of the battlespace. PSYOP provide a commander the means to employ a nonlethal capability across the range of military operations from peace through conflict to war and during post-conflict operations. As information delivered for effect during peacetime and conflict, PSYOP inform and influence. When properly employed, PSYOP saves lives of friendly and adversary forces, whether military or civilian. PSYOP may reduce the adversaries' will to fight, morale, and efficiency. PSYOP discourages aggressive actions, and creates dissidence and disaffection within their ranks, ultimately inducing surrender.

ROLES OF PSYOP

1-7. To execute their mission, PSYOP Soldiers perform the following five traditional roles to meet the intent of the supported commander:

- *Influence foreign populations* by expressing information subjectively to influence attitudes and behavior, and to obtain compliance, noninterference, or other desired behavioral changes. These actions facilitate military operations, minimize needless loss of life and collateral damage, and further the objectives of the supported commander, the United States, and its allies.
- *Advise the commander* on PSYACTs, PSYOP enabling actions, and targeting restrictions that the military force may execute. These actions and restrictions minimize adverse impacts and unintended consequences, attack the enemy's will to resist, and enhance successful mission accomplishment. PSYOP Soldiers also advise the commander on the psychological effects and consequences of other planned military actions and operations.
- *Provide public information* to foreign populations to support humanitarian activities, restore or reinforce legitimacy, ease suffering, and maintain or restore civil order. Providing public information supports and amplifies the effects of other capabilities and activities such as civil-military operations (CMO).
- *Serve as the supported commander's voice* to foreign populations to convey intent and establish credibility. This ability allows the commander to reach more audiences with less expenditure in resources and time.
- *Counter enemy propaganda, misinformation, disinformation, and opposing information* to portray friendly intent and actions correctly and positively for foreign TAs, thus denying others the ability to polarize public opinion and political will against the United States and its allies.

The role of psychological operations (PSYOP) in the information age is to assist military commanders in articulating their mission objectives, to help identify the decision makers who can promote or interfere with these objectives, and to recommend appropriate courses of action to properly influence them. In this regard, PSYOP is applicable across the operational continuum because command objectives may vary at any point in time and because key decision makers exist at every level of military endeavor... By converting command objectives into the people who have the ability to act on them, and by recommending the use of available military and nonmilitary resources, PSYOP soldiers attempt to educate and motivate targeted decision makers to act, or refrain from acting, in ways that support the commander's objectives.

Colonel Robert M. Schoenhaus,
7th PSYOP Group Commander, June 1999

POLICIES AND STRATEGIES

1-8. U.S. national policies and strategies seek to resolve conflict and deter hostilities. U.S. national policies and strategies have consistently had as their goal solutions to regional and international conflicts involving DIME approaches. When these attempts have given way to open hostilities, U.S. policy and strategy seeks quick resolution with minimal loss of life and destruction of property and infrastructure. A fundamental key to implementing these strategies and policies is building international support, often through broad-based coalitions. Another primary key to this strategy is influencing the leadership and key groups within foreign countries. At times, it has been the policy of the United States to appeal directly to foreign populaces, rather than to the tyrannical elites or unresponsive dictators who rule over them. This approach is applicable throughout the entire range of operations from peace through conflict to war. PSYOP can be not only a powerful arm of this strategy but also the only appropriate weapons system in the pre-conflict environment. PSYOP are a powerful nonlethal fire throughout an escalating conflict. There are, however, slight differences in the way the United States Government (USG) employs PSYOP at each level within full-spectrum operations. The types of PSYOP are as follows:

- *PSYOP at the strategic level* are the delivery of information to transregional TAs in support of U.S. goals and objectives. USG departments and agencies plan and conduct strategic-level information. Although many of the products and activities conducted are outside the arena of military PSYOP, Department of Defense (DOD) assets are frequently used in the development, design, production, distribution, and dissemination of strategic-level products. During peacetime, PSYOP forces often take part in operations that are joint, interagency, and multinational in nature. USG departments and agencies coordinate and integrate at the national level to conduct joint, interagency, and multinational operations. PSYOP assets can be a major contributor to missions, such as counterterrorism (CT), that have strategic implications.

- *PSYOP at the operational level* are conducted in support of the combatant commander's mission accomplishment. Along with other military operations, PSYOP may be used independently or as an integral part of other operations throughout the theater to support joint operations mission accomplishment. USG and DOD assets do operational-level PSYOP; however, DOD assets are the mainstay of operational PSYOP.
- *PSYOP at the tactical level* are used to support the maneuver commander's ability to win battles and engagements. PSYOP are conducted as an integral part of multinational, joint, and single-Service operations. Army special operations forces (ARSOF) assets conduct the overwhelming majority of tactical PSYOP.

PSYOP CORE TASKS

1-9. To meet the intent of the supported commander, PSYOP Soldiers perform six core tasks:

- *Develop.* Development involves the selection of Psychological Operations objectives (POs) and supporting Psychological Operations objectives (SPOs), the conceptualization of multiple series, the development of specific product ideas within a series, and the recommendation of actions that will influence the beliefs and attitudes of TAs and ultimately modify their behavior. In the development stage, PSYOP Soldiers conceptualize how they will modify behavior. The development stage combines several essential elements, including target audience analysis (TAA), series development, individual product development, and the approval process. The analysis of propaganda and the development of counterpropaganda begin during development but are embedded throughout the other core tasks.

- *Design.* Design is the technical aspect of taking what was conceptualized in the development stage and creating an audio, visual, or audiovisual prototype. This task demands technical expertise in many communication fields.
- *Produce.* Production is the transformation of approved PSYOP product prototypes into various media forms that are compatible with the way foreign populations are accustomed to receiving information. Some production requirements may be contracted to private industry, while other requirements may be performed by units attached or under the tactical control (TACON) or operational control (OPCON) of PSYOP forces.
- *Distribute.* Distribution is the movement of completed products from the production source to the point of dissemination. This task may include the temporary physical or electronic storage of PSYOP products at intermediate locations. This task can be complicated by classification requirements, as products are often classified before dissemination.
- *Disseminate.* Dissemination involves the delivery of PSYOP products directly to the desired TA. PSYOP forces must leverage as many different media and dissemination means as possible to ensure access to the targeted foreign population.
- *Evaluate.* Evaluation is the most resource-intensive of all PSYOP tasks. This task requires PSYOP Soldiers to integrate into the intelligence and targeting process. Evaluation includes analysis of impact indicators, surveys, interviews, and posttesting to measure the effectiveness to which PSYOP are achieving their objectives.

COMMAND AUTHORITY OF PSYOP FORCES

1-10. Upon approval of the SecDef, and direction of the Joint Chiefs of Staff (JCS), PSYOP forces are placed under the combatant command of the supported geographic combatant commander. The POTF commander may be designated as functional component commander directly subordinate to the geographic combatant commander or CJTF. The supported force operations officer (S/G/J/C3) exercises staff supervision of PSYOP forces.

1-11. PSYOP forces can work directly for the President and/or the SecDef, CJCS, U.S. Ambassadors, and other government agencies (OGAs). Before hostilities begin, the geographic combatant commander works closely with the Department of State (DOS) to ensure unity of effort and commonality of message. The DOS controls all information until an execute order for the PSYOP plan is approved. During this period before the execute order, and consistent with geographic combatant commander guidance, the DOS retains product approval authority while C2 remains in military channels. During peacetime PSYOP, the U.S. Ambassador is the command authority of any PSEs working in the host nation (HN).

1-12. Multipurpose dissemination platforms, such as the transportable amplitude modulation (AM)/frequency modulation (FM) radio broadcast system (TARBS) of the fleet information warfare center (FIWC), remain under OPCON of their Service component. The POTF exercises TACON to disseminate the supported commander's message responsively. However, the Air Force special operations component (AFSOC) EC-130E/J (known as COMMANDO SOLO) may be under OPCON of either the air component command or the joint special operations air component commander (JSOACC) of the joint special operations task force (JSOTF) and TACON to the PSYOP force.

1-13. When operating in joint, interagency, and multinational environments, a POTF or PSE will be under the command of the designated commander of DOD assets or the U.S. Ambassador. Currently, there is no overarching interagency doctrine that dictates relationships and procedures in interagency operations. Military organizations taking part in joint, interagency, and multinational operations must be mindful that the interagency process has been described as "more art than science." For further details concerning interagency coordination, refer to JP 3-08, *Interagency Coordination During Joint Operations, Volumes I and II.*

PSYOP APPROVAL AUTHORITIES

1-14. By U.S. policy and the PSYOP annex to the Joint Strategic Capabilities Plan (JSCP), product approval authority for PSYOP can be no lower than the CJTF. It is impossible to segregate the impacts of military and non-military PSYOP. The effects of public statements and actions of military and political leaders cross over DIME boundaries. For this reason, PSYOP objectives approval authority remains at levels where the interagency process is institutionalized (Figure 1-1).

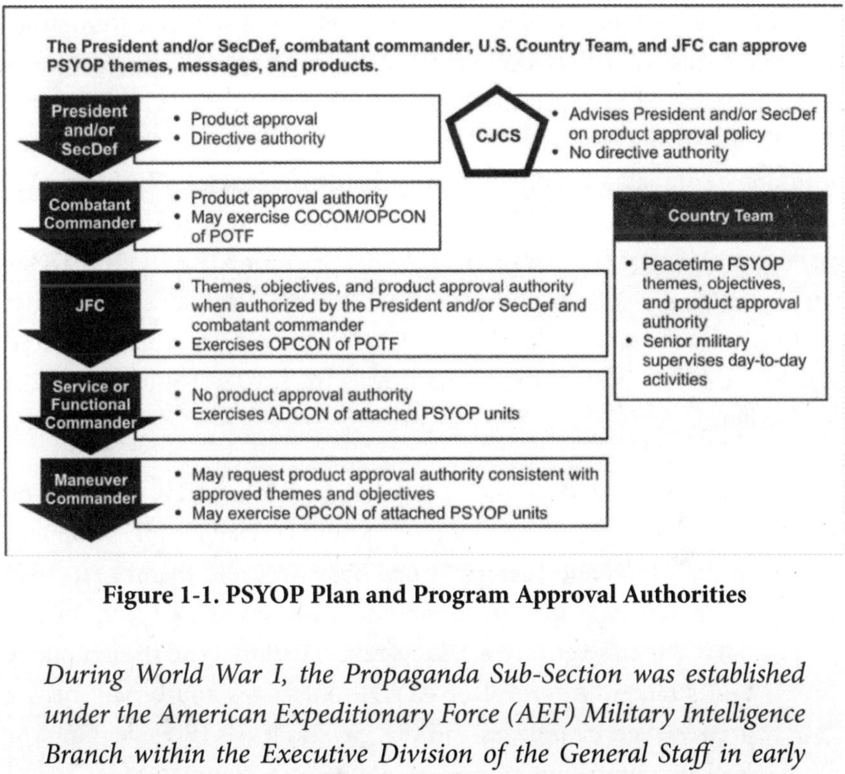

Figure 1-1. PSYOP Plan and Program Approval Authorities

During World War I, the Propaganda Sub-Section was established under the American Expeditionary Force (AEF) Military Intelligence Branch within the Executive Division of the General Staff in early 1918. Although they produced most propaganda, the AEF Propaganda Sub-Section did not produce a few of the leaflets. General Pershing is supposed to have personally composed Leaflet "Y," Austria Is Out of the War, which was run off on First Army presses, but distributed by the Propaganda Sub-Section. That Sub-Section, perhaps reflecting some professional jealousy, thought the leaflet sound in principle, but too prolix and a little too "brotherly." Corps and Army presses issued several small leaflet editions containing a "news flash," after the Sub-Section had approved their content. But in one or two cases that approval was not obtained, and in one unfortunate example a leaflet in Romanian committed the Allies and the United States to the union of all Romanians in Austria-Hungary with Romania. Such geo-politics was emphatically not the job of AEF propaganda and had the potential to cause serious embarrassment.

USASOC History Office

1-15. The SecDef normally delegates PSYOP approval authority to the supported geographic combatant commander in the JCS execution order and, in accordance with (IAW) the JSCP, the geographic combatant commander retains PSYOP approval authority following the approval of the PSYOP plan by the President and/or SecDef. During a crisis, the supported geographic combatant commander may, in turn, delegate PSYOP approval authority to the designated CJTF and even down to a maneuver commander, with SecDef approval. In the case of Operation IRAQI FREEDOM during the posthostilities phase, the SecDef authorized PSYOP product approval down to division level. In all PSYOP activities, commanders need to be aware of two levels of PSYOP approval. The two levels and differences are as follows:

- *Themes and PSYOP objectives.* The key to centralized planning and decentralized execution of PSYOP is clarity in the statement of objectives and themes. Broad objectives and themes establish the parameters for the development of series that reach foreign TAs. They also ensure products reflect national and theater policy and strategy. Approval of PSYOP objectives and broad themes are reserved by policies and the JSCP at levels (President and/or SecDef, combatant command, joint force command [JFC], and U.S. Country Teams) where the interagency process can invest PSYOP plans with a broad range of considerations.
- *Series.* A series is all the PSYOP products and actions to change one behavior of one target audience. Commanders subordinate to CJTFs can use approved series in order to achieve their specific objectives. CJTFs can also modify existing series or develop new series as long as the designated approval authority approves them.

There are three categories of products associated with PSYOP and/or propaganda: white, gray, and black (Appendix A). Military PSYOP most commonly use white products by policy and practice. CJTF commanders must carefully consider the approval authority for gray and black products due to the risk to credibility they present. The parameters for what tactical PSYOP forces can develop, design, produce, and disseminate will be articulated in the PSYOP support plan or subsequent orders.

1-16. The Country Team member designated by the U.S. Ambassador exercises approval authority for PSYOP forces deployed in support of U.S. Country Teams under the auspices of peacetime PSYOP as outlined in the JSCP. This representative is normally the deputy chief of mission (DCM), with reviewing authority to appropriate Country Team members, such as the public affairs officer (PAO) (until 1 October 1999, known as the Director, U.S. Information Service) and the Drug Enforcement Administration (DEA) representative.

1-17. Several possibilities exist, however, for approval authority if U.S. PSYOP forces are assigned OPCON to the multinational command under the command of a non-U.S. commander for the purpose of developing multinational products only (that is, no U.S. information products). PSYOP approval authority could remain with the geographic combatant commander, could be delegated to the senior U.S. military officer or diplomatic official involved in the operation, or could be further delegated to the non-U.S. commander (only with SecDef approval).

1-18. PSYOP must then be decentrally executed if they are to have a relevant and timely persuasive appeal. Tactical PSYOP forces in the field need the ability to conduct the PSYOP process if they are to provide flexible and responsive PSYOP support to the maneuver commander. The tactical Psychological Operations development detachment (TPDD) can use any series approved at the JTF level. The TPDD has the ability to develop, design, and produce series that accomplish SPOs, such as force protection or civilian noninterference, without these series being approved at the JTF level. This ability, however, must be approved in the initial plan signed by the SecDef. Tactical PSYOP forces can always develop series outside those specified parameters; however, they must go through the same approval process as POTF-level series. This process can include the addition of new products or the modification of existing products within an approved series.

SPECIAL CONSIDERATIONS

1-19. Army special operations (SO) imperatives are the guiding principles in the employment of SOF. Although the imperatives may not apply to all types of ARSOF, SOF commanders must include the applicable imperatives in their mission planning and execution. The Army SO imperatives are as follows:

- *Understand the operational environment.* ARSOF cannot dominate their environment without first gaining a clear understanding of the theater, including civilian influence, as well as enemy and friendly capabilities.
- *Recognize political implications.* Many SO are conducted to advance critical political objectives. ARSOF must understand that their actions can have international consequences.
- *Facilitate interagency activities.* ARSOF support and complement U.S. and multinational civilian programs driven by nonmilitary considerations. ARSOF can also operate in the ambiguous and complex political environments found in coalition operations or alliances formed to avert situations that would lead to human tragedy.
- *Engage the threat discriminately.* ARSOF are a limited resource that cannot be easily replaced. ARSOF mission objectives require careful application of when, where, and how.
- *Consider long-term effects.* ARSOF must consider the political, economic, informational, and military effects when faced with dilemmas, since the solutions will have broad, far-reaching effects. ARSOF must accept legal and political constraints to avoid strategic failure while achieving tactical success.
- *Ensure legitimacy and credibility of SO.* Significant legal and policy considerations apply to many SO activities. Legitimacy is

the most crucial factor in developing and maintaining internal and international support. The concept of legitimacy is broader than the strict legal definition contained in international law. The people of the nation and the international community determine its legitimacy based on collective perception of the credibility of its cause and methods. Without legitimacy and credibility, SO will not gain the support of foreign indigenous elements, the U.S. population, or the international community. ARSOF legal advisors must review all sensitive aspects of SO mission planning and execution.

- *Anticipate and control psychological effects.* All SO have significant psychological effects, some specifically produced and some based on perceptions. ARSOF must integrate PSYOP and public affairs (PA) into all their activities, anticipating and countering propaganda and disinformation themes to allow for maximum control of the environment.
- *Apply capabilities indirectly.* The primary role of ARSOF, in multinational operations, is to advise, train, and assist indigenous military and paramilitary forces. All U.S. efforts must reinforce and enhance the effectiveness, legitimacy, and credibility of the supported foreign government or group.
- *Develop multiple options.* ARSOF must maintain their operational flexibility by developing a broad range of options.
- *Ensure long-term sustainment.* ARSOF must demonstrate continuity of effort when dealing with political, economic, informational, and military programs. ARSOF must not begin programs that are beyond the economic, technological, or cultural capabilities of the HN to maintain without U.S. assistance. SO policy, strategy, and programs must therefore be durable, consistent, and sustainable.
- *Provide sufficient intelligence.* SO depend upon detailed, timely, and accurate intelligence. ARSOF must identify their information requirements (IRs) in priority.
- *Balance security and synchronization.* Insufficient security may compromise a mission. Excessive security will almost always cause the mission to fail because of inadequate coordination.

CAPABILITIES

1-20. U.S. Army PSYOP forces have the capability to produce print and broadcast media:

- *Print.* The mainstay of heavy print production assets is located at the media operation complex (MOC) at Fort Bragg, North Carolina. Deployable print systems can move multicolor print production to multiple theaters simultaneously. Through the use of organic and contract resources, U.S. Army PSYOP forces can produce materials ranging from leaflets and posters to commercial quality magazines. PSYOP forces have also produced national and regional newspapers.
- *Broadcast.* Several organic, deployable broadcast systems provide the capability to broadcast commercial band and shortwave (SW) radio and ultrahigh frequency (UHF) and very high frequency (VHF) television (TV) transmissions. Broadcast products ranging from short information spots to continuous broadcast of news and entertainment can be researched, produced, and disseminated by organic assets, HN assets, or platforms such as the EC-130E/J COMMANDO SOLO (Figure 1-2), a specially modified EC-130 possessing full-spectrum radio and TV broadcast ability.

Figure 1-2. EC-130E/J COMMANDO SOLO

1-21. Inherent in the force structure of PSYOP is a unique analytical capability. PSYOP Soldiers, enhanced by contracted native linguists, bring an in-depth knowledge of the culture, language, religion, values, and mindset of TAs within a country or region of operations. In addition, the strategic studies detachment (SSD) of 4th Psychological Operations Group (Airborne) (4th POG[A]) augments this capability with civilian regional experts.

1-22. Several organic near-real-time data transmission platforms support the reachback concept. Through use of digital links from home station to theater, reachback reduces the footprint of Soldiers deployed forward. A large research, design, and production team operating at a rear location can support smaller numbers of Soldiers functioning as distributors and disseminators in-theater. Under reachback, products are transmitted digitally to a forward team of minimal size from the team in the continental United States (CONUS) or at another intertheater or intratheater location.

ORGANIZATIONS

1-23. PSYOP forces are assigned to the United States Army Civil Affairs and Psychological Operations Command (USACAPOC), a major subordinate command of United States Army Special Operations Command (USASOC), at Fort Bragg. The Active Army forces are organized under the 4th POG(A) into four regional PSYOP battalions, a tactical PSYOP battalion, a dissemination battalion, and the SSD.

1-24. The majority of PSYOP units are in the Reserve Component (RC). Two additional PSYOP groups, the 2d and 7th Psychological Operations groups (POGs), provide tactical and dissemination battalions to support worldwide contingencies and exercises. The 2d and 7th POGs are each comprised of three tactical PSYOP battalions and a dissemination battalion.

1-25. In peacetime, RC PSYOP personnel will actively participate with Active Army PSYOP personnel in an integrated planning and training program to prepare for regional conflicts or contingencies. The RC can also be involved with the Active Army in the planning and execution of peacetime PSYOP programs. In wartime, the Service, as required by combatant commanders and constrained by national policy to augment Active Army PSYOP forces, may mobilize RC PSYOP assets. The RC can also continue peacetime PSYOP programs in the absence of Active Army PSYOP forces when mobilized or directed by higher authority. The RC can task, organize, mobilize, and deploy a PSYOP task group or POTF should a second regional conflict or contingency occur.

LEGAL ASPECTS OF PSYOP

1-26. U.S. law and policy, along with international conventions, regulations, and treaties, delineate the boundaries of PSYOP activity. These directives provide the following fundamental and practical guidelines for the conduct of PSYOP. Increasingly, military operations, such as Operation JOINT ENDEAVOR, are often multinational and involve contact with civilians, presenting greater legal and ethical issues with which to deal.

- *U.S. public law.* Title 10, United States Code (USC), Section 167, *Unified Combatant Command for Special Operations Forces,* designates PSYOP as an SO activity or force.
- *Presidential executive order.* DOD implementation policies of Executive Order S-12333, *United States Intelligence Activities*; DOD Instructions S-3321.1, (S) *Overt Psychological Operations Conducted by the Military Services in Peacetime and in Contingencies Short of Declared War* (U); and National Security Decision Directive (NSDD) 130, *U.S. International Information Policy*, direct that U.S. PSYOP forces will not target U.S. citizens at any time, in any location globally, or under any circumstances. However, commanders may use PSYOP forces to provide public information to U.S. audiences during times of disaster or crisis. The precedent for the limited use of PSYOP forces to present public information to a U.S. audience was set during the aftermath of Hurricane Andrew in 1992. Tactical Psychological Operations teams (TPTs) were employed to disseminate information by loudspeaker on locations of relief shelters and facilities. Information support to a noncombatant evacuation operation

(NEO) by PSYOP forces to provide evacuation information to U.S. and third-country nationals would also adhere to the order.

- *Geneva and Hague Conventions.* These international conventions preclude the injury of an enemy with actions of bad faith during his adherence to the law of war. PSYOP personnel will ensure that PSYOP activities do not contribute to such actions. PSYOP planners must work closely with the Judge Advocate General (JAG) to ensure that PSYOP support to deception does not violate the fourth Hague Convention that prohibits ruses that constitute "treachery" or "perfidity." Another chief concern of PSYOP is the treatment of enemy prisoners of war (EPWs). It is a violation of the Geneva Convention to publish photographic images of EPWs. PSYOP products must refrain from using images of actual EPWs. PSYOP planners must be prepared to advise commanders on potentially unlawful PSYOP lines of persuasion involving EPWs. Appendix B provides more information on internment/resettlement (I/R) operations.
- *Treaties in force.* International agreements with host countries may limit the activities of PSYOP units. Status-of-forces agreements (SOFAs) may seriously curtail employment of PSYOP in a HN. Of unique concern to PSYOP is the employment of any broadcast that might reach a third country. The SOFA agreements in place with multiple nations may need to be reviewed for some series. In addition to treaties already in force, the DOS or individual Country Teams in HNs may impose specific higher restrictions on the use of PSYOP contingent upon heightened states of tensions.
- *Within the HN or the region of the HN other statutory constraints may apply.* Postal regulations, specific regulations on propaganda, airspace or maritime agreements, and communications agreements may apply to PSYOP.
- *Rules of engagement (ROE).* ROE determine boundaries for PSYOP and PSYOP support to information operations. This method is particularly true for stability operations and support operations (SOSO), because of the presence of civilians and other factors. Therefore, PSYOP planners and commanders **must** fully understand ROE limitations. PSYOP planners must evaluate

ROE and analyze and anticipate the cultural and political aspects of not only a violation of the ROE by U.S. or HN forces but also compliance with the ROE. Appendix C provides more information on ROE.

- *Domestic laws.* Copyright law is an essential concern of PSYOP. No product may contain copyrighted material without consent by the copyright holder. If an image, sound file, logo, or any piece of media is used in a product, all copyright issues must be resolved before production.
- *Fiscal law.* Consumer goods used to transmit a line of persuasion (such as imprinted T-shirts or soccer balls) may present unique fiscal constraints. Procurement of such products on the economy in HNs may not be permitted with funds from some sources. In addition, use of HN assets may require adherence to contractual law that is dramatically different from U.S. law.
- *Communications.* U.S., HN, regional, and international communication agreements and protocols must be adhered to when conducting peacetime PSYOP. Constraints may continue to apply during hostilities. ROE may further constrain broadcasts.

Chapter 2

PSYOP MISSION AND INSTRUMENTS OF NATIONAL POWER

The mission of PSYOP is to influence the behavior of foreign TAs in support of U.S. national objectives. This mission gives PSYOP an important role in the exercise of all instruments of national power, including diplomatic, information, and economic measures, as well as military operations. The application of national power always contains a psychological dimension because the instruments of power are used to affect the decisions and ultimately the behavior of world leaders. The USG uses all of these instruments simultaneously in varying proportions. PSYOP has a unique capability to increase the effectiveness of the instruments of national power when properly focused. This chapter clarifies the ways in which PSYOP has traditionally supported the different instruments of national power. The breadth and variety of PSYOP approaches will likely increase as nontraditional threats continue to emerge.

PSYOP IN SUPPORT OF DIPLOMATIC MEASURES

2-1. According to the national security strategy, the USG relies on the armed forces to defend America's interests, but it must rely on public diplomacy to interact with other nations. The DOS takes the lead in managing the nation's bilateral relationships with other governments. Diplomatic efforts attempt to reach long-term political settlements that are in the best interest of the United States. DOD supports USG strategic communications activities with PSYOP in the form of military support to public diplomacy and military PSYOP.

2-2. PSYOP has traditionally supported public diplomacy by supporting ambassadors and Country Teams with small PSEs. Support is provided for many diplomatic efforts, including counterdrug (CD), humanitarian mine action (HMA), and peace building operations. These operations are often a cooperative effort between the USG and the HN, thus establishing important international ties. PSYOP support to diplomacy is integrated as part of the theater security cooperation plans (TSCP) that support regional security efforts.

2-3. During CD operations, PSYOP personnel focus on reducing the flow of illicit drugs into the United States. They do this by striving to achieve the following objectives:

- Decreasing the cultivation of illegal narcotic crops.
- Decreasing production and trafficking of drugs.
- Increasing the number of tips received about illegal drug activities.
- Reducing popular support for the drug trade.

2-4. PSYOP supporting CD operations augment diplomatic and economic efforts in support of the national security strategy by helping to reduce support for illegal drug production and trafficking as a means of livelihood in impoverished nations. Reduction of the drug trade weakens the drug cartels and reduces the levels of violence and corruption. Ultimately these efforts enhance the health and security of the United States.

2-5. HMA operations attempt to decrease casualties due to mines and unexploded ordnance (UXO). This is often accomplished by focusing on the dangers of mines, mine recognition, and what to do when a mine is encountered, leading to a decrease in mine-related injuries. PSYOP personnel can also train HN personnel on the establishment and running of national demining campaigns. PSYOP support to HMA operations helps further diplomatic efforts by providing assistance to HNs that may lack the experience or resources to mount a national-level mine awareness campaign.

2-6. Peace building operations consist of postconflict actions, predominantly diplomatic and economic, that strengthen and rebuild governmental infrastructure and institutions in order to avoid a relapse into conflict. In this role PSYOP often works in conjunction with Civil Affairs (CA) in publicizing the building of roads, wells, and schools. PSYOP is also instrumental, as is CA, in the reestablishing or creating of viable governmental entities.

2-7. These types of operations are commonly conducted to support the USG diplomatic efforts. The coordination and working relationships established with DOS entities is critical in the achievement of long-term diplomatic objectives.

PSYOP IN SUPPORT OF INFORMATION MEASURES

2-8. Military PSYOP support USG informational efforts under the auspices of military support to public diplomacy (MSPD). In this role military PSYOP may work closely with the Bureau of International Information Programs (IIP) under the DOS. Because military PSYOP (known at the interagency level as international military information [IMI]) play a major role in international public information, the impact of interagency information efforts on PSYOP planning is significant. It is therefore important for PSYOP planners to understand not only the interagency environment and mindset, but also the criticality of interagency coordination.

2-9. The projection of targeted information to foreign audiences by the USG is becoming a very important instrument of national power. Consequently, as the use of targeted international information in support of U.S. policy objectives increases, so too does the role of military PSYOP in support of interagency information efforts.

2-10. An example of military PSYOP in support of public diplomacy or international information was when the joint Psychological Operations task force (JPOTF) helped in building and maintaining international support for the military effort in Northern Iraq after the first Gulf War. By conducting thoroughly planned and executed international information programs, the USG was able to successfully project information that promoted and explained U.S. policy. Aggressive information programs on the international level are absolutely necessary in influencing world political opinion and communicating U.S. efforts to foreign audiences.

PSYOP IN SUPPORT OF MILITARY OPERATIONS

2-11. The effect of military operations can be magnified by PSYOP through the modification of the behavior of foreign TAs. It is important for the military commander to remember that any mission given to PSYOP cannot be accomplished simply by the production and dissemination of a few PSYOP products. It can only be accomplished by convincing the TA of a series of arguments that lead to the desired behavioral change.

2-12. PSYOP supports both offensive and defensive operations. The PSYOP process is essentially identical for both offensive and defensive operations. The end state of both offensive and defensive operations is to hasten the eventual defeat of enemy forces by—

- Undermining the will of the enemy to resist.
- Increasing unrest among the civilian population in enemy areas.
- Increasing desertion or surrender of enemy forces.
- Reducing civilian interference with military operations.
- Undermining the credibility of enemy leadership.
- Reducing damage to elements of infrastructure critical to end-state objectives.
- Increasing acceptance of friendly forces in occupied territory.
- Deterring intervention of neutral and neighboring powers.
- Countering propaganda.

Any of these objectives can be supported by PSYOP at the operational and tactical levels. Some specific methods of how PSYOP supports offensive and defensive operations are discussed in Chapter 8 of FM 3-05.301.

2-13. PSYOP also supports SOSO around the world. They promote and protect U.S. national interests by influencing the threat, political, and information dimensions of the operational environment. They include developmental and cooperative activities during peacetime and coercive actions in response to crisis. Army forces accomplish stability goals through engagement and response. The military activities that support stability operations are diverse, continuous, and often long-term. Their purpose is to promote and sustain regional and global stability. Examples of PSYOP support during stability operations include CT, NEOs, foreign internal defense (FID), unconventional warfare (UW), and humanitarian assistance (HA).

COUNTERTERRORISM

2-14. PSYOP supports CT by integrating with other security operations to target the forces employing terrorism. The aim is to place the terrorist forces on the psychological defensive. To do so, PSYOP forces analyze the terrorists' goals and use psychological programs to frustrate those goals. PSYOP forces support CT by—

- Countering the adverse effects of a terrorist act.
- Decreasing popular support for the terrorist cause.
- Publicizing incentives to the local populace to provide information on terrorist groups.

2-15. CT operations are complex and necessitate cooperation between many agencies and across geographic regions, as terrorism has become a worldwide phenomenon.

NONCOMBATANT EVACUATION OPERATIONS

2-16. NEOs are conducted to remove USG personnel, citizens, and approved third-country nationals from areas of danger. PSYOP units support these operations by reducing interference from friendly, neutral, and hostile TAs and by providing information to evacuees.

FOREIGN INTERNAL DEFENSE

2-17. FID programs encompass the total political, economic, informational, and military support provided to another nation to assist its fight against subversion and insurgency. PSYOP support to FID focuses on assisting HN personnel to anticipate, preclude, and counter these threats. FID supports HN internal defense and development (IDAD) programs. U.S. military involvement in FID has traditionally been focused on helping another nation defeat an organized movement attempting to overthrow the government. U.S. FID programs may address other threats to a HN's internal stability, such as civil disorder, illicit drug trafficking, and terrorism. These threats may, in fact, predominate in the future as traditional power centers shift, suppressed cultural and ethnic rivalries surface, and the economic incentives of illegal drug trafficking continue. PSYOP support FID programs through direct support to HN governments facing instability as well as training opportunities through the joint combined exercise for training (JCET) program.

UNCONVENTIONAL WARFARE

2-18. All military operations have a psychological impact, and a major component of UW is the psychological preparation of the area of operations (AO). PSYOP units are a vital part of UW operations. When properly employed, coordinated, and integrated, they can significantly enhance the combat power of resistance forces. PSYOP specialists augmenting the Special Forces operational detachments (SFODs) can deploy into any joint special operations area (JSOA). These PSYOP specialists through TAA identify the conditions, vulnerabilities, lines of persuasion, susceptibilities, accessibilities, and impact indicators of foreign TAs that will support U.S. objectives. PSYOP in contemporary and future UW become more critical as ideological and resistance struggles increase.

HUMANITARIAN ASSISTANCE

2-19. HA operations are conducted to provide relief to victims of natural and man-made disasters. PSYOP units support these operations by providing information on benefits of programs, shelter locations, food and water points, and medical care locations. PSYOP units also publicize HA operations to build support for the U.S. and HN governments.

SUPPORT OPERATIONS

2-20. The last type of operation conducted by military forces is support operations. These operations use military forces to assist civil authorities, foreign or domestic, as they prepare for or respond to crises and relieve suffering. In support operations, military forces provide essential support, services, assets, or specialized resources to help civil authorities deal with situations beyond their capabilities. The purpose of support operations is to meet the immediate needs of designated groups for a limited time, until civil authorities can do so without military assistance. An example of a PSYOP operation in this category is disaster relief. PSYOP in the past has used loudspeakers to provide disaster relief information to victims or make announcements in a camp scenario.

PSYOP IN SUPPORT OF ECONOMIC MEASURES

2-21. The USG promotes a strong world economy in an attempt to enhance our national security by advancing prosperity and freedom in the rest of the world. Economic growth supported by free trade and free markets creates new jobs and higher incomes. It allows people to lift their lives out of poverty, spurs economic and legal reform and the fight against corruption, and reinforces the habits of liberty.

2-22. By being one of the world's strongest economies, the USG can leverage its economic standing as an instrument of national power. An example of an economic measure is the establishment of exclusion zones. They prohibit specified activities in a specific geographic area. Exclusion zones can be established in the air (no-fly zones), sea (maritime), or on land. The purpose may be to persuade nations or groups to modify their behavior to meet the desires of the sanctioning body or face continued imposition of sanctions, or the threat of force. The United Nations (UN), or other international bodies of which the United States is a member, usually imposes economic measures. They may, however, also be imposed unilaterally by the United States. Exclusion zones are usually imposed due to breaches of international standards of human rights or flagrant abuse of international law regarding the conduct of states. The sanctions may create economic, political, military, or other conditions where the intent is to change the behavior of the offending nation. PSYOP supports economic measures by participating in such operations as Operation SOUTHERN WATCH over Iraq after the first Gulf War. PSYOP has also been an important part of several maritime interdiction operations (MIO), including Operation ENDURING FREEDOM and Operation IRAQI FREEDOM.

2-23. The instruments of national power are exercised continually by the USG to promote U.S. policy worldwide. PSYOP supports many diplomatic, informational, military, and economic measures to help the USG achieve its objectives. PSYOP is a core task of the United States Special Operations Command (USSOCOM) and therefore a change in national security strategy or policy may add, delete, or alter the nature of PSYOP.

Chapter 3

ORGANIZATION, FUNCTION, AND CAPABILITIES

This chapter addresses the PSYOP force—the structure of units by which USASOC executes PSYOP missions. Creating and maintaining this structure is under administrative control (ADCON) of the Department of the Army and USSOCOM. This chapter explains the functions, capabilities, and organization of U.S. Army PSYOP units.

PSYOP GROUP

3-1. A POG is a multipurpose and extremely flexible organization that commands organic and attached elements conducting PSYOP. Figure 3-1 shows the organization of an Active Army POG. Figure 3-2, page 28, shows the organization of a RC POG. A POG plans, coordinates, and executes PSYOP at the strategic, operational, and tactical levels in support of the President and/or SecDef, combatant commanders, and OGAs as directed by the SecDef. It can establish, operate, and support up to two POTFs at the combatant command and JTF level. An Active Army POG consists of a group headquarters and headquarters company (HHC), regional Psychological Operations battalions (POBs), a tactical POB, a dissemination POB, and an SSD. An RC POG consists of a group HHC, tactical POB, and a dissemination POB. A POG is structured to support conventional forces and SOF. The President and/or SecDef require at least one airborne POG to support global requirements.

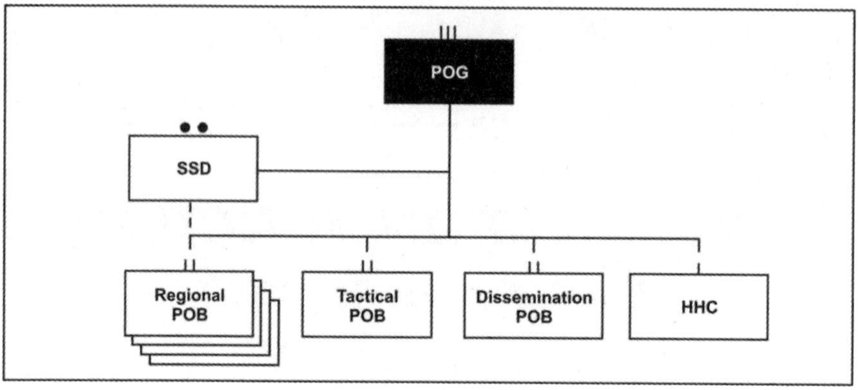

Figure 3-1. Active Army POG

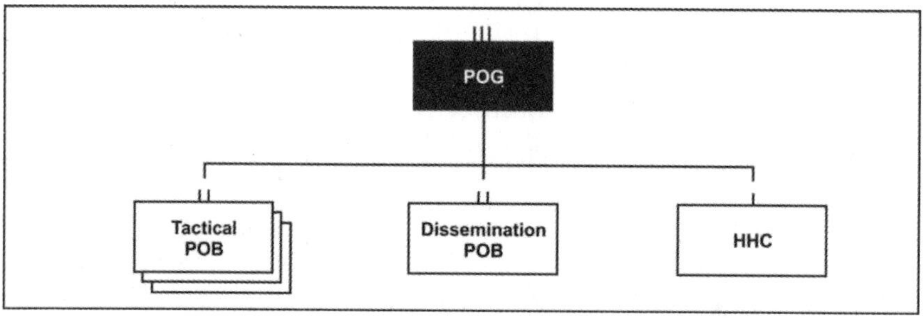

Figure 3-2. RC POG

HEADQUARTERS AND HEADQUARTERS COMPANY

3-2. The group HHC provides C2, staff planning, and staff supervision of group operations and administration.

COMMAND GROUP

3-3. The *group commander* exercises command of a POG and all attached elements. When a POTF is established, the POG commander designates the PSYOP task force commander.

3-4. The *deputy commanding officer* (DCO) performs those duties assigned by the group commander, to include directing the day-to-day activities and command of the POG in the commander's absence.

3-5. The *executive officer* (XO) is the principal member of the group staff. He functions in a manner similar to a chief of staff. The XO directs, coordinates, and integrates the activities of the group staff.

PERSONAL STAFF GROUP

3-6. The *command sergeant major* (CSM) is the group's senior noncommissioned officer (NCO). He is the principal advisor to the commander and staff on matters pertaining to enlisted personnel and the NCO corps as a whole. He monitors policy implementation and standards on the performance, training, appearance, and conduct of enlisted personnel. He provides counsel and guidance to NCOs and other enlisted Soldiers.

3-7. The *chaplain* is the personal staff officer who coordinates the religious assets and operations within the command. The chaplain is a confidential advisor to the commander for religious matters.

3-8. The *Staff Judge Advocate* (SJA) is the commander's personal legal advisor on all matters affecting the morale, good order, and discipline of the command. As a special staff officer, the SJA provides legal support to the command and the community. As a member of a PSYOP command, the SJA pays special attention to the laws, policies, conventions, regulations, and treaties that guide the conduct of PSYOP.

COORDINATING STAFF GROUP

3-9. The *S-1* is the primary staff officer for all matters concerning personnel. His specific duties are manning operations, casualty operations, and health and personnel service support. Other duties include headquarters (HQ) management, staff planning, and coordination for specific chaplain and SJA functions.

3-10. The *S-2* is the principal staff officer for all matters pertaining to intelligence. His specific areas of responsibility are military intelligence (collecting and disseminating intelligence), counterintelligence, and military intelligence training. The S-2 plans for the collection, processing, and dissemination of intelligence that is required for POG activities. He advises the commander in the use of POG intelligence assets and provides the S-3 with intelligence support for the operations security (OPSEC) program and deception planning.

3-11. The *S-3* is the key staff officer for matters pertaining to the overall operations of the POG. His areas of responsibility are primarily training and current operations.

3-12. The *S-4* is the primary staff officer for all logistics matters. His specific areas of responsibility are logistics operations, plans, and transportation. The S-4 has staff planning and supervision over battlefield procurement and contracting, real property control, food service, fire protection, bath and laundry services, clothing exchange, and mortuary affairs.

3-13. The *S-6* is the key staff officer for all communications matters. His specific duties involve automation and network management, coordination for signal support external to the POG, strategic communications, and telephone operations.

SPECIAL STAFF GROUP

3-14. The *deputy commanding officer for research, analysis, and civilian affairs* (DCO-RACA) manages the PSYOP studies and intelligence research programs that support all PSYOP groups and their subordinate elements. His specific duties are to represent the commander in the intelligence production cycle, direct special projects and analytical responses to contingencies and special actions, supervise intelligence research by civilian analysts, and manage all programs pertaining to civilians. As directed, he conducts special projects assigned by the group commander.

3-15. The *resource management officer* (RMO) is the special staff officer for budget preparation and implementation and resource management analysis. His specific responsibilities include preparing the command operating budget and program objective memorandum. The RMO also oversees cost capturing for operations.

REGIONAL PSYOP BATTALION

3-16. A regional POB has the same fundamental capabilities found in the POG—it plans and conducts PSYOP (Figure 3-3, below). It is common for a regional POB commander to be designated as the PSYOP component commander, functional component commander, or POTF commander in peacetime and to continue this role in wartime (if a POG does not assume the mission). Each geographic combatant commander requires at least one dedicated regional POB.

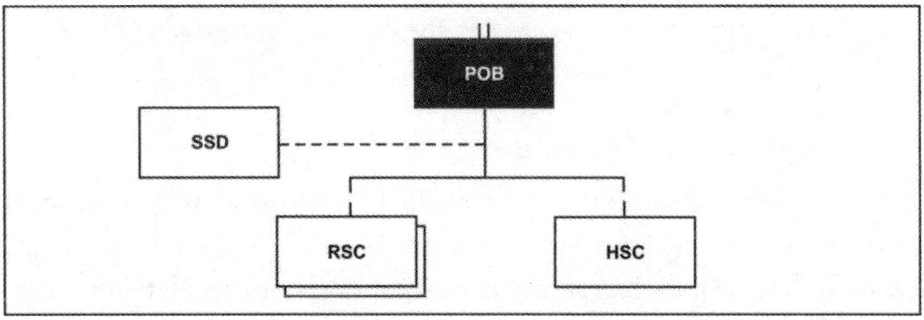

Figure 3-3. Regional POB

HEADQUARTERS AND SUPPORT COMPANY

3-17. The regional battalion headquarters support company (HSC) functions similarly to the HSCs in other units. It provides resources and supervision to the staff and oversees operations and administration of the battalion as a whole.

3-18. The *XO* is the principal member of the battalion staff. He functions in a manner similar to a chief of staff. The XO directs, coordinates, and integrates the activities of the battalion staff and commands the battalion in the commander's absence. The regional POB CSM has the same duties and responsibilities as the group CSM.

3-19. The *regional POB staff* differs from the POG staff in that it does not have an RMO, SJA, chaplain, or S-6. The following paragraphs explain two other important characteristics.

3-20. The *regional POB S-2* has the same responsibilities as the POG S-2. In addition, the regional POB S-2 coordinates the sampling of TAs by the interrogation sergeant in the S-2 section.

3-21. *SSD chiefs* are the supervisory intelligence research specialists and intelligence experts in PSYOP for the regional POB. Specific duties are supervising the analysts assigned to a regional POB; managing the research and production activities; developing new PSYOP concepts, guidelines, applications, and methodologies; and reviewing and editing PSYOP intelligence documents.

3-22. There is no *S-6* in the regional POB. The support company of the dissemination POB provides communications support as required.

REGIONAL SUPPORT COMPANY

3-23. The regional support company (RSC) conducts PSYOP in support of the overall plan (Figure 3-4). There may be two product development centers (PDCs) in each regional POB. The PDCs design, develop, manage, and review PSYOP products and programs. The subordinate elements of the PDC are normally organized along functional lines. Some regional support companies choose to merge the four functional capabilities into operational detachments.

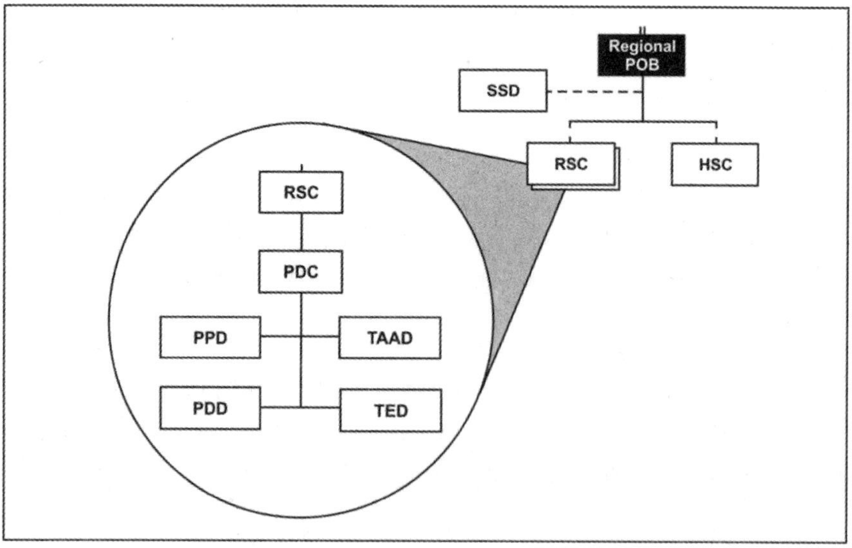

Figure 3-4. RSC

Plans and Programs Detachment

3-24. The plans and programs detachment (PPD) manages the PSYOP process (Chapter 6) and is solely responsible for Phase I, III (with input from other sections), V, and portions of Phase VII of the PSYOP process. The PPD is the operational center of the PDC. The PPD conducts mission analysis and assists the G-3 in developing the PSYOP tab/appendix to the combatant commander/JFC's campaign plan. The POTF operations section manages Phase VI.

Target Audience Analysis Detachment

3-25. The target audience analysis detachment (TAAD) is responsible for Phase II of the PSYOP process. It refines the potential target audience lists (PTALs) and analyzes them as they relate to a given SPO. TAAD members combine efforts with SSD personnel to complete detailed target audience analysis work sheets (TAAWs).

Product Development Detachment

3-26. The product development detachment (PDD) is responsible for Phase IV of the PSYOP process. The PDD develops and designs PSYOP series. The PDD has the ability to design audio, visual, and audiovisual products according to input from other PDC sections. The PDD monitors and coordinates product development. This detachment organizes internal meetings and the PDD work panel to produce the product concepts and prototypes. The PDD work panel usually includes representatives from each PDC section and print, broadcast, signal, and SSD elements.

Testing and Evaluation Detachment

3-27. The testing and evaluation detachment (TED) is responsible for the majority of Phase VII. The TED develops pretests and posttests to evaluate PSYOP impact on TAs. The TED obtains feedback from TAs, including EPWs, civilian internees (CIs), and displaced civilians (DCs) through interviews, interrogations, surveys, and other means to further assess impact and to get feedback and determine PSYOP-relevant intelligence. The TED may also assist POTF elements with translation tasks.

Strategic Studies Detachment

3-28. An SSD supports each regional POB. The SSD is made up entirely of Army civilian PSYOP analysts who provide area expertise, linguistic skills, and an organic social research capability to the regional POB. Most analysts have an advanced degree, and all read and speak at least one of the languages in their area of expertise. SSD analysts write the PSYOP portions of the Department of Defense Intelligence Production Program (DODIPP) and produce several different PSYOP-specific studies. The analysts participate in deliberate and contingency planning and deploy to support operations.

TACTICAL PSYOP BATTALION

3-29. The tactical POB provides support to all Services at corps, JTF-level and below (Figure 3-5, page 35). It also supports select SO or conventional task forces at Army-level equivalent-sized units. The battalion staff and elements of the companies can conduct planning and operations at the component operational level.

3-30. The tactical POB can develop, produce, and disseminate series within the guidance (themes, objectives, and TAs) assigned by the POTF and authorized by the PSYOP approval authority. Any series developed that do not fall within assigned guidelines must be submitted to the POTF for approval.

3-31. When the tactical POB deploys in support of a maneuver unit, they are normally task-organized with assets from a dissemination POB. At the battalion level, the tactical POB is generally task-organized with a theater support team from the dissemination battalion's signal company, which provides product distribution and C2 support. This team may consist of: four personnel; a vehicle with trailer; a product distribution system (PDS); an international maritime satellite-B (INMARSAT-B) earth station to provide commercial satellite communications capability for encoding, compressing (Motion Pictures Expert Group [MPEG]-1 format), and distributing audio and video data; and appropriate tactical communications systems for C2 (single-channel tactical satellite [TACSAT] and FM). In addition, the team may be equipped to establish a local area network (LAN) using the PDS for internal communications within the tactical POB HQ.

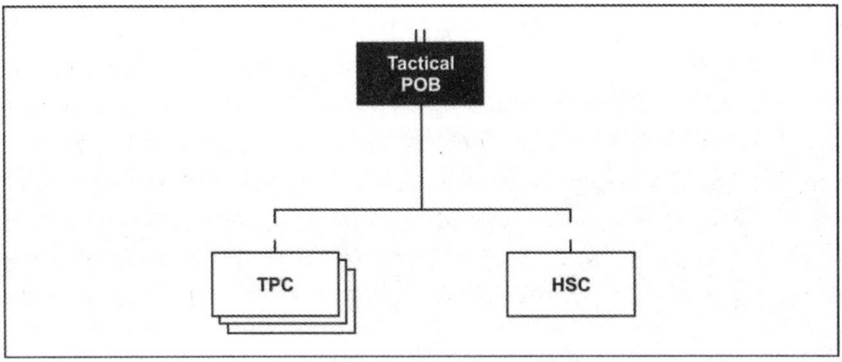

Figure 3-5. Tactical POB

HEADQUARTERS AND SUPPORT COMPANY

3-32. The tactical battalion HSC provides similar functions and capabilities as other HSCs. It focuses on support to staff and supporting elements within the company.

3-33. The tactical POB commander exercises command of the battalion and all attached elements. The tactical POB XO has the same duties and responsibilities as the regional POB XO. The tactical POB CSM has the same duties and responsibilities as the group CSM. The tactical POB coordinating staff group has the same duties and responsibilities as the POG coordinating staff.

TACTICAL PSYOP COMPANY

3-34. The tactical Psychological Operations company (TPC) is the centerpiece of PSYOP support to ground commanders (Figure 3-6, page 36). The level of PSYOP support required ranges from one TPC per division/SF group in high-intensity conflict to as much as one TPC per brigade/regiment/Special Forces (SF) battalion in SOSO. The higher level of support in SOSO is determined by the need to influence the larger urban population generally found within a static brigade/regiment/SF battalion sector. In recent operations population densities in brigade-equivalent sectors ranged from 500,000 (Kosovo Peacekeeping Force [KFOR]) to 2+ million (Operation IRAQI FREEDOM [OIF]). Supported units include Active Army and RC divisions/brigades, Marine expeditionary force (MEF)/divisions/ Marine expeditionary battalion (MEB)/Marine expeditionary unit (MEU), battalions/companies, military police brigades/battalions conducting I/R operations, and air security squadrons. Support elements are tailored to provide PSYOP staff planning and to conduct tactical PSYOP support. The TPC has limited product development and production capability. For PSYOP support beyond the TPC's capabilities, coordination is made through the higher-echelon PSE to the POTF, or directly to the POTF if a higher-echelon PSE is not deployed.

3-35. The TPC is normally task-organized with assets from the broadcast and print companies of the dissemination battalion. This support may include a flyaway broadcast system (FABS) or a Special Operations Media System-Broadcast (SOMS-B) to provide the TPC a direct support (DS) broadcast asset. In addition, each TPC may be task-organized with a Deployable Print Production Center (DPPC) from the print company of the dissemination battalion. This tactical vehicle-mounted, light print asset provides the TPC with a responsive and mobile digital print capability. The TPC is then able to produce limited PSYOP products, such as leaflets, handbills, posters, and other printed material (within the guidance assigned by the POTF and authorized by the approval authority).

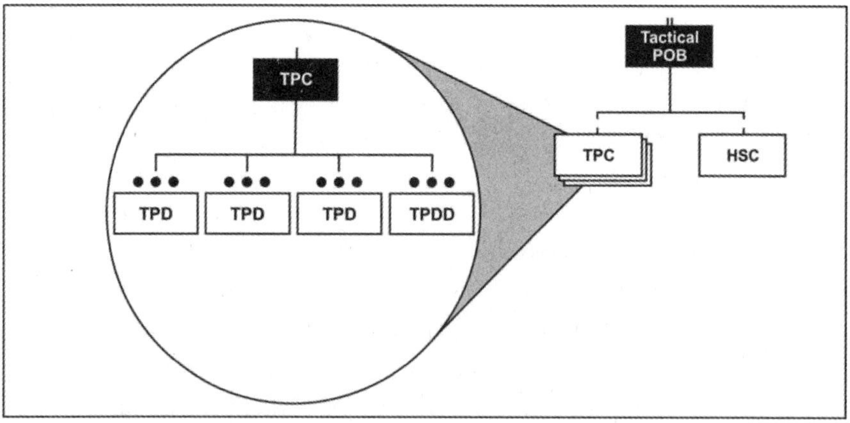

Figure 3-6. TPC

Tactical Psychological Operations Development Detachment

3-36. The TPDD is normally colocated with the TPC and provides the supported commander with responsive PSYOP support (Figure 3-7, below). The TPC normally has one TPDD that coordinates closely with the supported unit's staff to conduct the PSYOP process. The TPDD synchronizes and coordinates PSYOP by subordinate or attached elements. The TPDD also provides PSYOP support to any tactical Psychological Operations detachments (TPDs) providing support to I/R operations. The TPDD is usually located with the supported unit's HQ.

3-37. The TPDD has an organic MSQ-85B. This multimedia production and development asset gives the TPC the capability to provide the maneuver commander with timely, responsive, and effective PSYOP products.

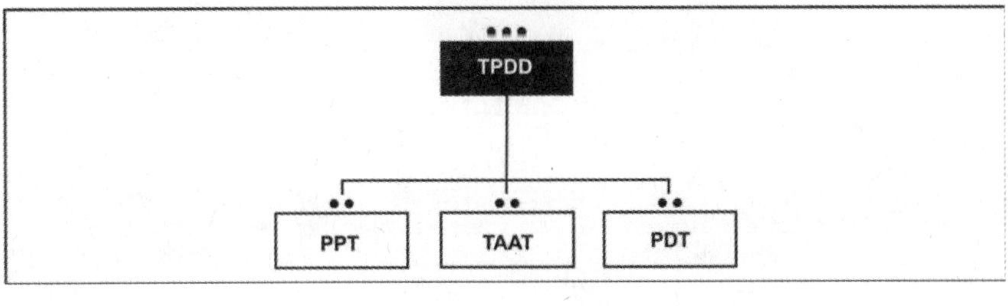

Figure 3-7. TPDD

Tactical Psychological Operations Detachment

3-38. In high-intensity conflict the TPD normally provides PSYOP support to a brigade-size element or equivalent, such as a MEU, an SF battalion, a Ranger regiment, a special mission unit, an armored cavalry regiment, a Stryker Brigade, an MP battalion responsible for an I/R facility, or a separate infantry regiment or brigade (Figure 3-8, page 38). Due to the need to influence the larger urban population densities sometimes present in static unit sectors in SOSO, the TPD can support a battalion or equivalent-sized unit. The TPD analyzes the higher-HQ operation order (OPORD) and the associated PSYOP tab or appendix (Appendix 2 [PSYOP] for Army OPORDs/operation plans (OPLANs) and Tab D [PSYOP] to Annex P [Information Operations] to Annex C [Operations] for Joint OPORDs/OPLANs) to determine specified and implied PSYOP tasks. These tasks are subsequently incorporated into the supported unit PSYOP annex. These PSYOP tasks also are focused specifically on how they will support the scheme of maneuver. Therefore, the TPD commander normally recommends to the operations officer that he either retain his organic TPTs under TPD control or allocate them to subordinate units.

3-39. The TPD exercises staff supervision over TPTs allocated to subordinate units, monitoring their status and providing assistance in PSYOP planning as needed. Unlike the TPC, however, the TPD does not have any organic PSYOP product development capability. The TPD coordinates with the TPDD for the PSYOP capability required to accomplish the supported unit's mission. The focus of TPD planning is on integrating series dissemination to support the maneuver commander.

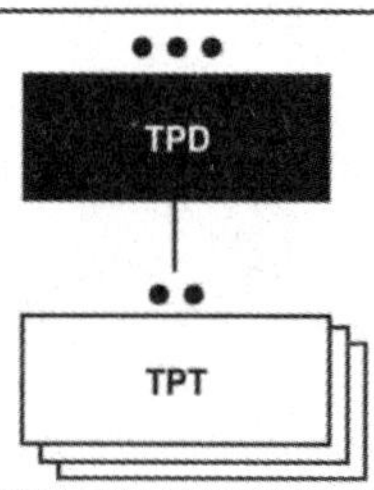

Figure 3-8. TPD

Tactical Psychological Operations Team

3-40. In high-intensity conflict the TPT normally provides PSYOP support to a battalion. Higher rates of movement during combat operations allow tactical commanders to reinforce units in contact with PSYOP assets as needed. During more static and/or urban SOSO, planning and execution of operations are primarily conducted at the company/Special Forces operational detachment A (SFODA) level, and the company/SFODA is the element that most often directly engages the local government, populace, and adversary groups. The company requires a more dedicated PSYOP capability to manage the population found in a company sector, particularly in urban environments when population densities are much higher (for example, 50,000 to 200,000 per company sector). Operating in the team or company AO allows the TPTs to develop rapport with the TAs. This rapport is critical to the accomplishment of their mission. The

TPT chief is the PSYOP planner for the supported commander. He also coordinates with the TPD for PSYOP support to meet the supported commander's requirements.

DISSEMINATION PSYOP BATTALION

3-41. The dissemination POB provides audio, visual, and audiovisual production support, product distribution support, signal support, and media broadcast capabilities to the PSEs (Figure 3-9). The dissemination POBs can simultaneously support two separate theaters at the combatant command level.

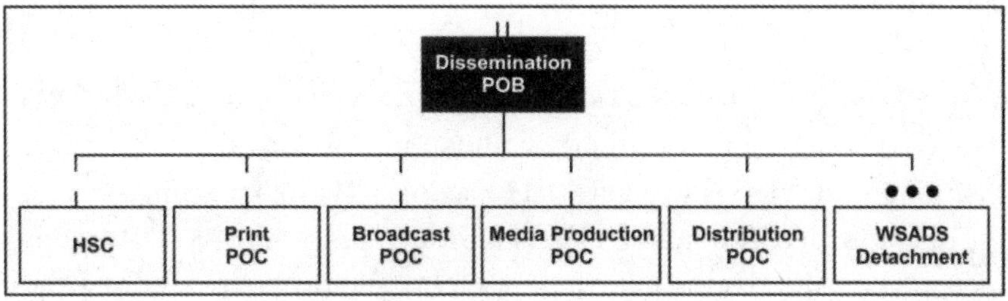

Figure 3-9. Dissemination POB

MEDIA OPERATIONS COMPLEX

3-42. The 3d POB (Dissem), 4th POG(A) operates the MOC at Fort Bragg, North Carolina. The MOC consolidates a heavy print facility, a media production center, a production distribution facility, an electronics maintenance shop, and a maintenance support team under one roof. This facility provides general support to PSYOP forces worldwide by means of satellite communications links that allow forward deployed forces to request and receive support. Print, audio, and audiovisual products developed in the MOC can be transmitted electronically for production and dissemination in forward locations.

HEADQUARTERS AND SUPPORT COMPANY

3-43. The dissemination battalion HSC provides C2 and maintenance support to deployed print, media, and support teams. It also provides maintenance support for the PSYOP group and its nondeployed organic elements.

3-44. The battalion commander exercises command of the battalion and all attached elements. The dissemination POB XO and CSM have the same duties as their counterparts in the regional and tactical POBs. The dissemination POB special staff group has the same responsibilities as the regional POB.

PRINT PSYCHOLOGICAL OPERATIONS COMPANY

3-45. The print Psychological Operations company (POC) (Figure 3-10, below) provides print, packaging, and leaflet dissemination support to PSEs. It uses a variety of print equipment from fixed digital presses to high-speed, deployable duplication machines. It also operates a variety of commercial equipment.

BROADCAST PSYCHOLOGICAL OPERATIONS COMPANY

3-46. The broadcast POC of the dissemination POB provides media broadcast support to the PSEs (Figure 3-11, page 41). It provides support across the operational continuum and in response to peacetime PSYOP requirements established by the joint staff or OGAs. Transmitter support ranges from lightweight, short-range transmitters to a vehicle-mounted system with organic production assets to long-range TV and radio platforms that

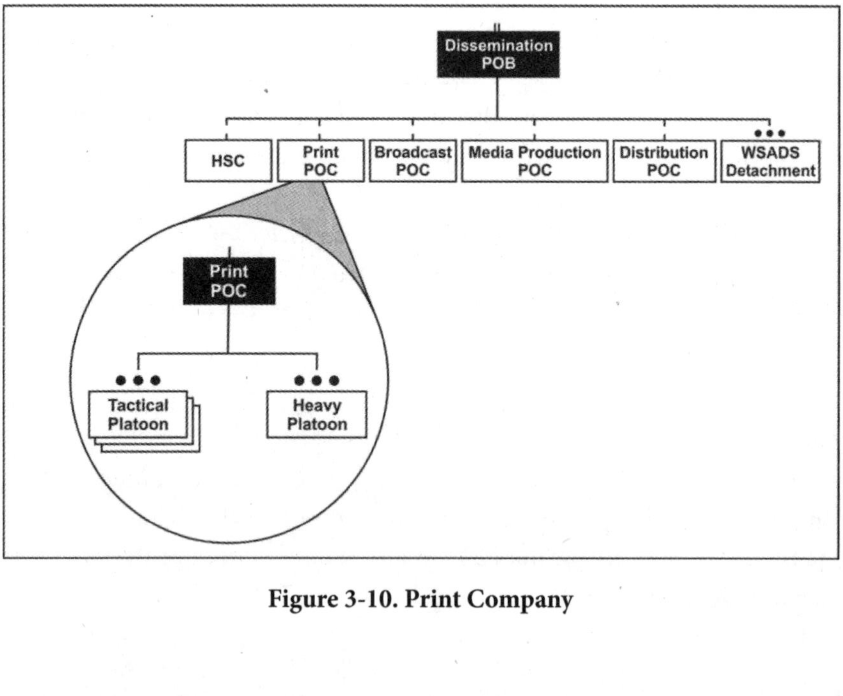

Figure 3-10. Print Company

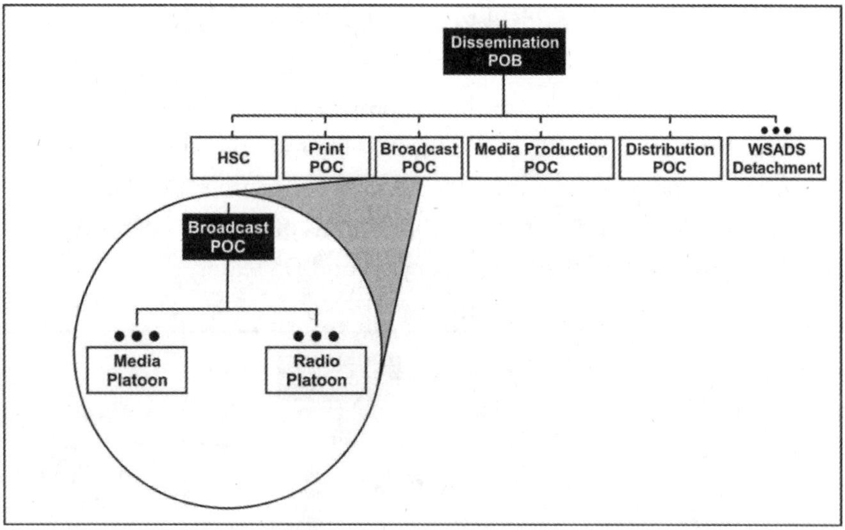

Figure 3-11. Broadcast POC

allow PSYOP programming to be broadcast deep into restricted areas to reach distant TAs. The broadcast POC deploys video camera teams with mobile editing equipment capable of producing high-quality audio and video PSYOP products. It can also provide limited intermediate DS/general support (GS) maintenance for organic and commercial broadcast for both radio and TV equipment.

MEDIA PRODUCTION PSYCHOLOGICAL OPERATIONS COMPANY

3-47. The Active Army media production POC has the capability to produce commercial-quality graphics, photographic, audio, and audiovisual products. This unit operates the fixed-station Media Production Center (MPC), located at Fort Bragg, North Carolina, as well as deploying Theater Media Production Centers (TMPCs) in support of the geographic combatant commanders (GCCs). The MOC is the media production and product archive hub for the PSYOP community and is critical to reachback employment. The MOC normally provides DS to combatant commanders or joint force commanders for the conduct of PSYOP during crisis operations. The MOC provides GS for the execution of international military information and peacetime PSYOP programs.

DISTRIBUTION PSYCHOLOGICAL OPERATIONS COMPANY

3-48. The distribution POC of the dissemination POB provides communications support to the POGs, POBs, POTFs, and other deployed PSEs in the form of product distribution and C2 assets (Figure 3-12). The PSYOP distribution POC provides support for all levels of military operations and task-organizes around the theater support and DS teams.

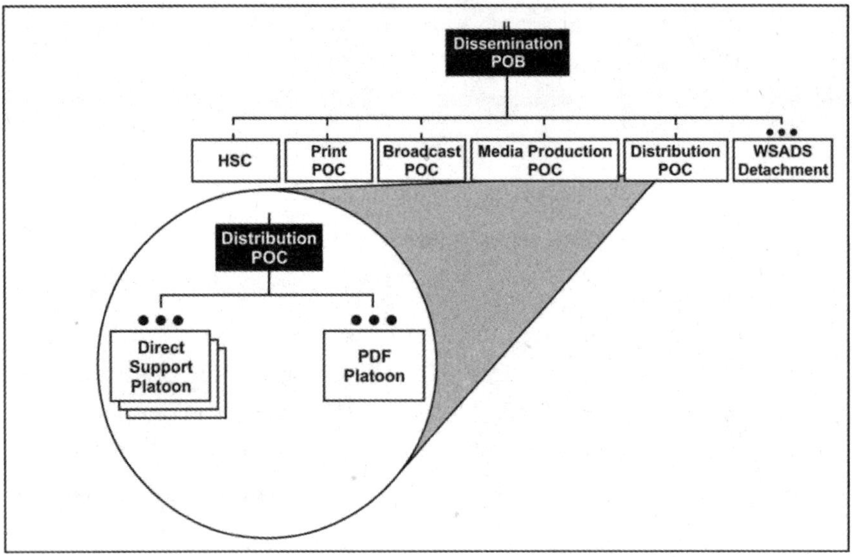

Figure 3-12. Distribution POC

3-49. The Active Army distribution POC also operates the product distribution facility (PDF). This is a dedicated facility for housing product distribution hardware that enables PSYOP units to distribute products throughout the world via SECRET Internet Protocol Router Network (SIPRNET) and into Europe via the Bosnia command and control augmentation (BC2A) system. The PDF also houses United Press International (UPI) downlink equipment, providing 24-hour access to PSYOP units.

WIND SUPPORTED AERIAL DELIVERY SYSTEM DETACHMENT

3-50. The CQ-10A "Snow Goose" unmanned aerial vehicle (UAV) is a versatile, ground launched, autonomously guided, parafoil system that has the ability to deliver leaflets to multiple targets in both permissive and denied airspace. Other variants of the system are being studied for possible development. The wind supported aerial delivery system (WSADS) detachment of the dissemination POB is a provisional organization whose purpose is to conduct operational employment evaluation of the WSADS, conduct familiarization training on the system, and provide support to PSYOP forces. This operational testing is to determine the operational and tactical applications of the system, develop tactics, techniques, and procedures (TTP) for its use and integration into air tasking orders (ATOs), and determine additional requirements to fully develop the capabilities of the system. Initial employment of the system involves attachment of the system and launch/recovery team to supporting PSYOP forces to provide a dedicated aerial dissemination capability from JPOTF through TPC level.

Chapter 4

COMMAND AND CONTROL

PSYOP may operate under various C2 arrangements. The mission, the length and scope of operations, the supported GCC, and the commanders at each level determine the exact C2 structure. PSYOP may be an integral part of joint or multinational operation, or an activity in support of OGAs. This chapter discusses the C2 structure as it relates to the Army PSYOP force. This discussion focuses on C2 arrangements and the command relationships developed to facilitate effective PSYOP support.

GENERAL

4-1. All PSYOP are essentially joint in scope given the level at which the approval of PSYOP programs occurs. In application, PSYOP support may extend from strategic to tactical levels. Regardless of the level at which PSYOP are applied, PSYOP planning is conducted at all levels. Under JP 3-53, PSYOP may be executed in a national, joint, combined, interagency or single-Service context. Commands that direct the use of PSYOP include unified or specified combatant commands, subordinate unified commands, and JTFs. The principles of war are the basis for joint PSYOP doctrine. These principles do not try to constrain the Service department additions or deletions. They are, however, the focal point for planning and executing PSYOP.

4-2. Effective PSYOP need a responsive C2 structure. The command relationship arrangements for C2 of PSYOP must—

- Provide a clear, unambiguous chain of command.
- Provide enough staff experience and expertise to plan, conduct, and support PSYOP.

- Ensure the supported commander involves selected PSYOP personnel in mission planning at the outset.

GENERAL STRUCTURE

4-3. The broad range of PSYOP requires that they be coordinated, synchronized, integrated, and deconflicted at all levels. However, to maximize their timeliness and tailor them to specific situations, commanders must plan and execute PSYOP at the lowest appropriate level, within the guidelines of general theater PSYOP guidance. Even though PSYOP fully support the activities of other SOF, the majority of missions are in support of the geographic theater combatant commander's overall campaign and conventional forces.

4-4. When the SecDef approves the deployment of PSYOP personnel to perform peacetime PSYOP activities in support of theater security cooperation plans (formerly the overt peacetime Psychological Operations [PSYOP] program–[OP3]), OPCON of these forces passes to the supported GCC. PSYOP personnel perform their mission under the supervision of the Country Team official designated by the U.S. Ambassador or Chief of Mission.

4-5. To effectively execute its mission, the POTF or JPOTF (if one is chartered) sets up as a separate functional component of the combatant commander or CJTF HQ. A JPOTF, as a JTF, may be established by the SecDef, a combatant commander, a subunified commander, a functional component commander, or an existing commander of a JTF (FM 100-7, *Decisive Force: The Army in Theater Operations*; JP 3-0, *Doctrine for Joint Operations*; JP 5-0, *Doctrine for Planning Joint Operations*; and JP 5-00.2, *Joint Task Force [JTF] Planning Guidance and Procedures)*. The POTF normally falls directly under the OPCON of the theater GCC or CJTF, and tactical or operational PSYOP forces are normally attached to the appropriate maneuver force commander.

4-6. When a POTF is deployed and the supported GCC is given OPCON of the POTF, the execute order will stipulate whether or not the GCC is authorized to subdelegate OPCON to a JFC. The POTF is responsible for providing PSYOP support to the overall joint or combined operation at the operational and tactical levels. It coordinates with each of the Service components, functional components, and staff elements to determine PSYOP requirements according to mission analysis. A PSE or a POAT may be OPCON to the U.S. Ambassador. Finally, it may coordinate strategic-level PSYOP with the combatant command and the joint staff through the appropriate command channels, as per the JSCP.

4-7. Mission requirements will determine the composition of a POTF. In many cases, the POTF may include forces from other Services or other coalition countries. Under these circumstances, the POTF may be chartered as a JPOTF or a combined JPOTF (sometimes referred to as a combined joint Psychological Operations task force [CJPOTF]). The command relationships in these cases are discussed in the remainder of this chapter.

4-8. Tactical POBs and TPCs are normally attached to armies, corps, divisions, brigades, or equivalent-sized elements. Dissemination PSYOP battalions normally operate as major subordinate units or detachments of the POTF.

4-9. Multipurpose assets that are primarily PSYOP platforms, such as EC-130E/J COMMANDO SOLO and other aerial platforms, usually remain under OPCON to their Service or functional component but are under TACON of the POTF. The POTF normally has coordinating authority over operational and tactical PSYOP units. This authority allows the POTF to augment tactical PSYOP units and coordinate the technical aspects of development, production, distribution, and dissemination of PSYOP to ensure unity of effort and adherence to GCC and CJTF plans. It is not a command relationship; rather, it is one of consultation. (JP 0-2, *Unified Action Armed Forces [UNAAF]*, discusses the relationship further.)

4-10. In the absence of a POTF or a JTF, the GCC normally exercises OPCON of the PSYOP forces through the commander of the United States military group (USMILGP), the security assistance office (SAO) chief, or the Defense Attaché Office (DAO). This intermediate commander then keeps the ambassador informed of plans and activities during the deployment.

OPERATIONAL CONTROL

4-11. The GCC may exercise OPCON, or he may delegate OPCON to any level of command subordinate to him. Inherent in OPCON are authorities similar to those contained in combatant command, command authority (COCOM). OPCON does not in and of itself include authoritative direction for logistics or matters of administration, discipline, internal organization, or unit training.

TACTICAL CONTROL

4-12. The GCC may exercise TACON or he may delegate it to any level of command subordinate to him. TACON does not include organizational authority or authoritative direction for administrative and logistic support. The establishing directive must define the specific authorities and limits of TACON.

COORDINATING AUTHORITY

4-13. PSYOP forces are habitually attached; therefore, coordinating authority between PSYOP elements is critical to synchronize and coordinate the PSYOP effort throughout all echelons. In the absence of coordination, contradictory PSYOP may occur, potentially compromising the effectiveness of the information operations effort.

UNITED STATES SPECIAL OPERATIONS COMMAND

4-14. USSOCOM is the unified combatant command for SO, including PSYOP (Figure 4-1, page 49). The SecDef assigns all CONUS-based PSYOP forces to the Commander, United States Special Operations Command (CDRUSSOCOM). He exercises COCOM of assigned forces through a combination of Service and joint component commanders. CDRUSSOCOM prepares assigned PSYOP forces to conduct PSYOP supporting U.S. national security interests across the operational continuum. Through the CJCS, and in coordination with the Assistant Secretary of Defense (Special Operations and Low Intensity Conflict) (ASD[SO/LIC]), he advises the President and/or SecDef and the National Security Council (NSC) on PSYOP matters. CDRUSSOCOM has no geographic area of responsibility (AOR) for normal operations. He normally acts as a supporting combatant commander, providing mission-ready PSYOP forces to GCCs for use under their COCOM. The President and/or SecDef may direct CDRUSSOCOM to command PSYOP forces as a supported combatant commander or to support an GCC. (JP 3-05, *Doctrine for Joint Special Operations*, has further information.)

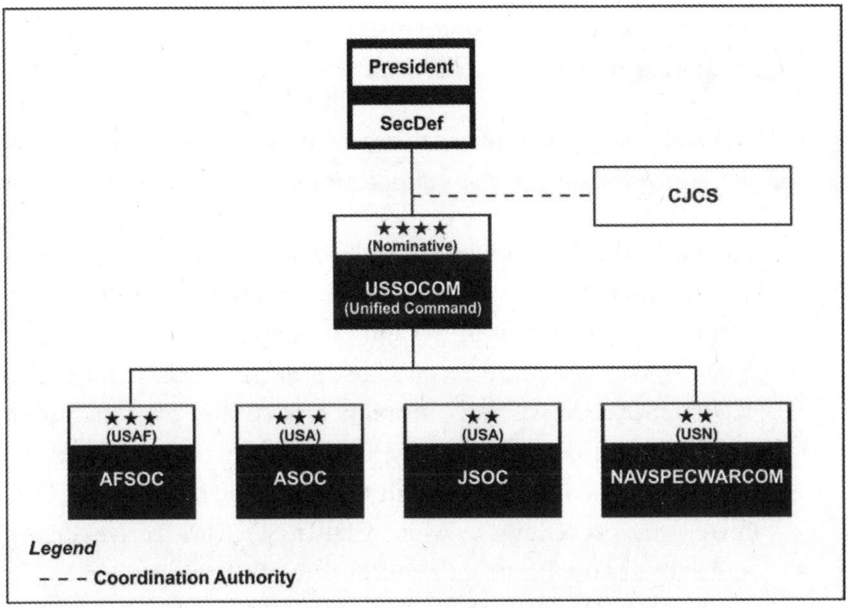

Figure 4-1. USSOCOM Command Relationships

4-15. Public law gives CDRUSSOCOM broad functional authority to carry out his responsibility for PSYOP forces. This authority includes—

- Developing joint PSYOP strategy, doctrine, and tactics.
- Educating and training assigned forces.
- Conducting special courses of instruction for officers and NCOs.
- Validating and ranking PSYOP requirements.
- Ensuring assigned forces are mission-ready.
- Developing and procuring PSYOP-specific materiel, supplies, and services.
- Ensuring the compatibility and interoperability of PSYOP equipment with the PSYOP forces.
- Instituting and implementing procedures for PSYOP intelligence support.

- Monitoring the promotions, assignments, retention, training, and professional military education of PSYOP personnel.
- Monitoring the preparedness of PSYOP forces assigned to other unified COCOMs.
- Combining and proposing PSYOP programs to Major Force Program 11 (MFP 11), a separate military funding program for PSYOP and SO.
- Preparing and executing MFP 11.

4-16. DOD staff has several offices that advise the SecDef in the area of special operations and low intensity conflict (SO/LIC). They are as follows:

- Subject to the direction of the SecDef, the *ASD(SO/LIC)* provides policy guidance and oversight to govern planning, programming, resourcing, and executing SO and LIC activities.
- The *Office of the Secretary of Defense* (OSD) staff and CDRUSSOCOM will have visibility and control over the use of MFP 11 resources. Additionally, among other responsibilities, the OSD staff, in coordination with the CJCS and CDRUSSOCOM, reviews the procedures by which CDRUSSOCOM receives, plans, and executes the President's and/or SecDef's taskings.
- With the OSD staff, the *CDRUSSOCOM* has head-of-agency authority. MFP 11 provides visibility and control of the PSYOP forces resource allocation process. The OSD staff and CDRUSSOCOM oversee the DOD Planning, Programming, and Budgeting System (PPBS) on PSYOP forces. They have the chance to address issues during sessions of the Defense Resources Board. The CDRUSSOCOM's Washington office is his command element in the Washington area. This office is USSOCOM's link with the Services, DOD, Congress, OGAs, and nongovernmental agencies for all PSYOP matters.

UNITED STATES ARMY SPECIAL OPERATIONS COMMAND

4-17. USASOC is a major Army command (MACOM) and the Army component command of USSOCOM (Figure 4-2, page 51). Its mission is to command, support, and ensure the combat readiness of assigned and attached Army forces for worldwide use. As a MACOM, it focuses on policy development, management and distribution of resources, and long-range planning, programming, and budgeting of ARSOF. The USASOC commander exercises command of CONUS-based Active Army and RC ARSOF. When directed by CDRUSSOCOM, USASOC provides

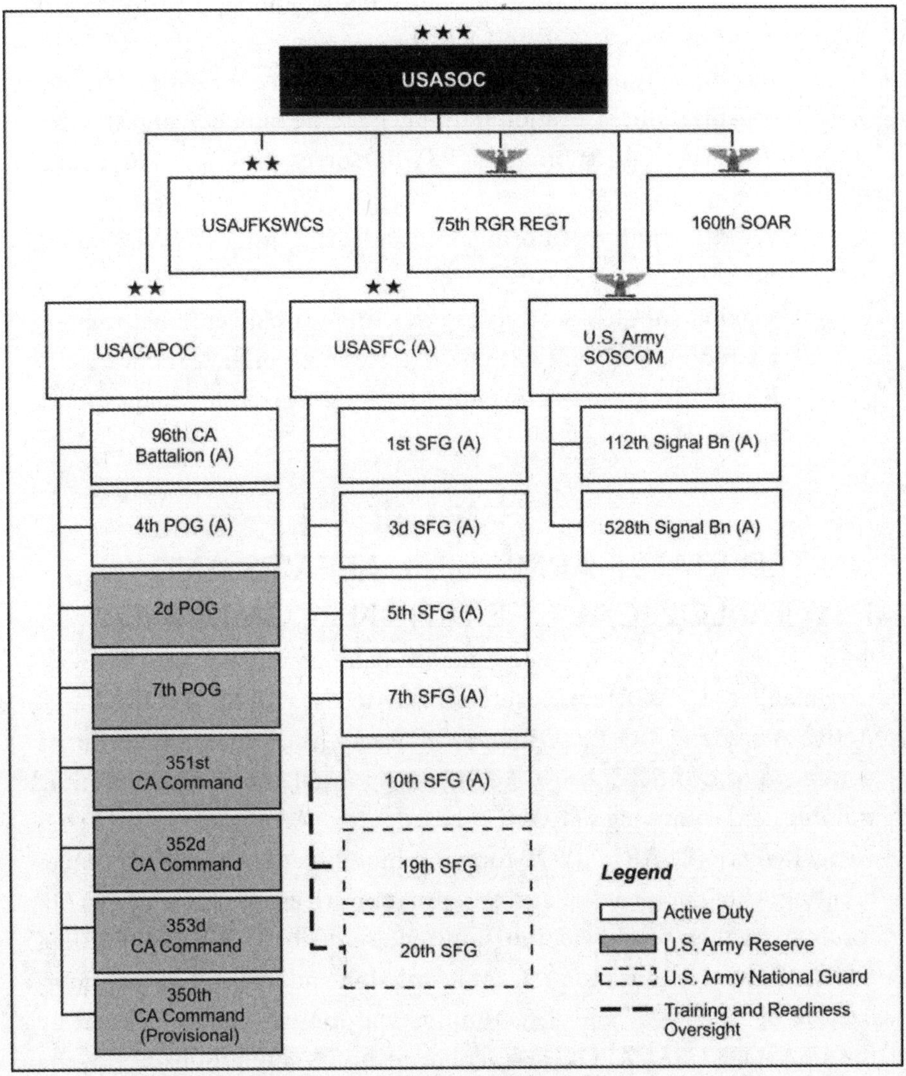

Figure 4-2. USASOC Organization

mission-ready PSYOP forces to the GCCs for use under their COCOM. Specific USASOC functions include—

- Training assigned forces to ensure the highest level of mission readiness consistent with available resources.
- Directing the planning and preparation of assigned ARSOF for contingency and wartime employment.
- Assisting in developing and coordinating joint and Army PSYOP requirements, issues, and activities.
- Assisting in developing joint and Army PSYOP doctrine, organization, institution training, materiel, supplies, and services.
- Preparing and submitting PSYOP forces program and budget documents.
- Coordinating, monitoring, and preparing forces for support of special activities.
- Making sure assigned forces can support conventional military operations and joint PSYOP in peacetime, conflict, and war.
- Planning and conducting other training, operations, and support, as directed.

UNITED STATES ARMY CIVIL AFFAIRS AND PSYCHOLOGICAL OPERATIONS COMMAND

4-18. USACAPOC is a major subordinate command of USASOC. Commander, USACAPOC, exercises day-to-day C2 of CONUS-based Active Army and RC PSYOP and CA forces. As a major subordinate command of USASOC, USACAPOC is responsible for the organization, training, and equipping of CONUS-based Active Army and United States Army Reserve (USAR) PSYOP forces. It monitors the progress of implementing ARSOF policies, plans, and programs to ensure CA and PSYOP forces meet their worldwide mission requirements. Upon mobilization, USACAPOC continues to perform its mission and to assist in the mobilization of USAR CA and PSYOP units and individuals, as directed by the USASOC. USACAPOC tasks subordinate PSYOP groups to execute missions. The Active Army PSYOP group (4th POG[A]), with subordinate PSYOP battalions apportioned to the geographic combatant commanders, functions as the mission planning agent of USACAPOC for all Active Army and RC PSYOP forces through the single-source PSYOP concept.

THEATER SPECIAL OPERATIONS COMMAND

4-19. The theater special operations command (TSOC) serves three functions for PSYOP forces in-theater: SO component command; Title 10 service, administration, and support; and, when directed by the theater GCC, warfighting. It specifically provides for the administrative and PSYOP-unique logistics support of PSYOP forces in-theater. A special operations theater support element (SOTSE) is attached by USASOC to the TSOC to coordinate logistics support for deployed PSYOP forces.

4-20. The TSOC exercises ADCON (joint term for what the Army designates "command less OPCON") of the PSYOP forces. It exercises OPCON of the assigned PSYOP force when—

- The PSYOP force is not chartered as a functional component command.
- The PSYOP force is not under the OPCON of another component command.

PSYCHOLOGICAL OPERATIONS TASK FORCE

4-21. The SecDef assigns or attaches all required PSYOP forces outside the continental United States (OCONUS) through USSOCOM to the supported GCC. Only the President and/or SecDef can authorize the transfer of COCOM from one GCC to another. The transfer of COCOM occurs when forces are reassigned. When forces are not reassigned, OPCON passes to the supported GCC. The President and/or SecDef (through JCS command arrangements) specifies in the deployment order when and to whom COCOM or OPCON passes.

4-22. The POTF (a task-organized PSYOP battalion operating independently) normally forms the basis for the senior PSYOP HQ in-theater (Figure 4-3, page 54). With appropriate augmentation, this HQ normally becomes a joint organization. This joint HQ is normally referred to as a JPOTF.

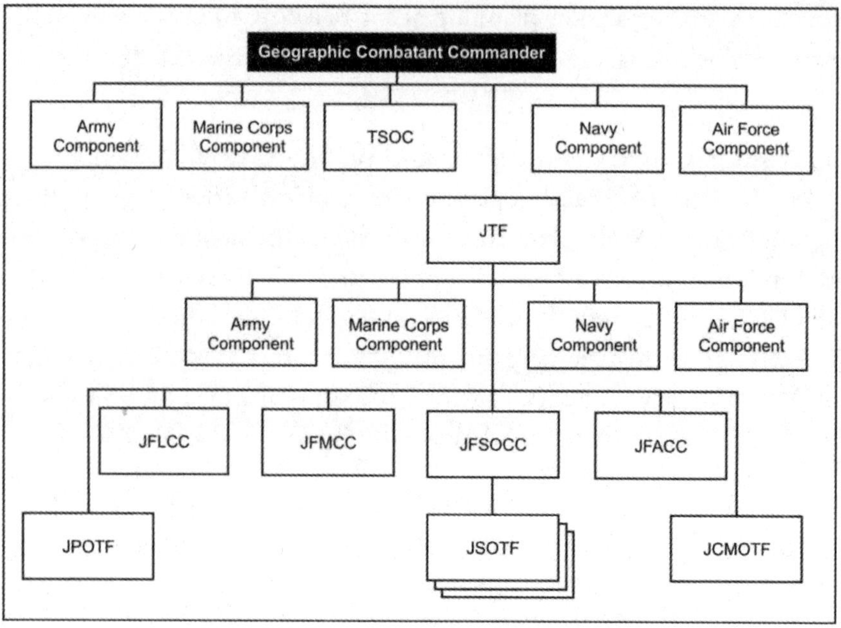

Figure 4-3. JPOTF in Joint Force Organization

4-23. The JPOTF is located with the senior commander in-theater. The JPOTF is with the GCC's HQ during war and the JPOTF with the task force HQ during a contingency operation. During a smaller contingency operation, the JPOTF will be with the commander of the JTF HQ (a sub-unified command or a component command in the absence of the GCC). The senior PSYOP commander in-theater supporting the warfighting GCC recommends organizational options to perform the PSYOP mission. The warfighting GCC approves one of the recommended options. These organizational options depend on the situation, mission, and duration of operations. The JPOTF controls all PSYOP.

4-24. The JPOTF normally fits into the unified command structure as a functional component command reporting directly to the GCC. The JPOTF normally provides PSYOP augmentation to the J-3 division as an integral part of the GCC's staff. In this case, the JPOTF commander wears two hats—he is the GCC's senior PSYOP staff officer and he is the commander of the JPOTF exercising OPCON over all PSYOP forces in-theater. The JPOTF normally functions the same way with a JTF. During peacetime and smaller contingency operations, the Active Army POG may only have to provide PSYOP augmentation to the GCC or JTF headquarters.

NOTE: All PSYOP C2 elements are dual-tasked as the principal staff member for PSYOP to their supported HQ.

4-25. PSYOP elements depend on their supported elements for routine sustainment. This relationship may be described as attached for administration and logistics (ADCON or command less OPCON). Their mission guidance continues to come through PSYOP channels to the supported unit. The theater Army special operations support command (TASOSC) ensures PSYOP sustainment requirements are properly planned for and coordinated with TA support elements. The JPOTF will perform this function in the absence of a TASOSC.

4-26. Establishment of a JPOTF at the COCOM level or senior headquarters level is essential during all major, high-visibility military operations conducted within the GCC's AOR, regardless of scope, duration, or degree of direct participation exercised by the GCC. The psychological impact of military operations conducted by a subordinate unified command or a JTF is never confined to the specific operational area. Rather, it creates a spillover effect that may be felt over large areas of the supported GCC's region and, in some cases, far beyond his geographic boundaries into an adjacent GCC's AOR. The JPOTF would, at the supported GCC's direction, plan and develop PSYOP programs to neutralize or reverse the negative psychological impact in the affected areas. These programs must be coordinated with the adjacent GCC's theaterwide PSYOP efforts to obtain the same response. The JPOTF C2 structure ensures a coordinated PSYOP plan to support the GCC's theater campaign plan.

4-27. The supported GCC's mission and the estimated duration of PSYOP activities influence the senior PSYOP commander's recommendation. Army PSYOP forces support conventional forces during conventional operations and SF performing SOF missions. The senior PSYOP commander assigns a liaison team to the special operations command (SOC) and JSOTF, if established.

4-28. The senior PSYOP commander in-theater, when supporting SO, recommends to the SOC or JSOTF commander the proper use of PSYOP to support SO. During contingencies, the senior PSYOP commander must analyze the supported GCC's mission and update the applicable PSYOP appendix. He then allocates PSYOP assets to support SO according to the mission, situation, and assets available. The JFC gives the SOC or JSOTF commander authority to accomplish assigned missions and tasks.

DEPLOYMENT

4-29. Upon receiving deployment orders, the PSYOP units move to a port of embarkation (POE). From there, they move by air or sea into the gaining GCC's AOR. At a predetermined point (for example, upon crossing a specified latitude or longitude), COCOM or OPCON is formally passed to the gaining GCC.

4-30. When a POTF exists, tactical and operational PSYOP forces should be attached to the POTF. The POTF commander then detaches tactical forces from the POTF and attaches them to the appropriate supported unit. Operational PSYOP forces remain under OPCON of the POTF. This allows the POTF commander to ensure that PSYOP forces are appropriately task-organized and gives the POTF the ability to centrally control and/or synchronize the PSYOP effort.

MULTINATIONAL OPERATIONS

4-31. The Joint Staff executes orders that may contain a provision allowing the gaining combatant commander to integrate PSYOP forces into multinational operations. For the purpose of developing non-U.S. products only, OPCON of U.S. PSYOP forces may pass to a non-U.S. commander. The command relations of PSYOP forces will generally be the same as other participating U.S. forces. The SecDef will normally transfer OPCON of PSYOP forces to the supported GCC in the execute order and may authorize him to transfer OPCON to the JFC, to the senior U.S. military officer involved in the operation, or to a non-U.S. commander.

A Combined Joint Task Force under CJ3 supervision was responsible for implementing the NATO psychological operations campaign. Under IFOR, the task force was called the Combined Joint IFOR Information Campaign Task Force (CJIICTF). With SFOR operations (20 December 1996), the name changed to Combined Joint Information Campaign Task Force (CJICTF). Both task forces were directed by U.S. Army Reserve Colonels, and were mainly composed of U.S. personnel and assets with supporting elements from France, Germany, and the United Kingdom...Political sensitivities not only made European nations reluctant to using PSYOP, but also complicated the command and control situation. From December 1995 to October 1997, U.S. PSYOP personnel (which formed the core of the CJIICTF) remained under national command and control. As a result of the 1984 National Security Decision Directive 130, the U.S. Department of Defense refused to place PSYOP forces under NATO command and control... The American refusal caused problems in everyday operations (such as coordination and logistics problems)... Finally, the U.S. refusal to place its PSYOP forces under NATO C2 caused tensions within the Alliance. European nations felt the PSYOP effort was not fully NATO and were therefore reluctant to become full participants...Finally in October 1997, the U.S. DOD transferred U.S. PSYOP forces in theater to SACEUR's command and control.

"Target Bosnia: Integrating Information Activities in Peace Operations" (Institute for National Strategic Studies, 1998) by Pascale Siegel

INTERAGENCY COORDINATION

4-32. Trends during recent operations and missions involving U.S. forces, particularly in civil activity at home and abroad, have indicated a propensity for not only joint and multinational cooperation and coordination, but also significant interagency involvement. Because this increased level of interagency and DOD cooperation is relatively new, lessons learned and planning considerations are not as widespread as they need to be.

LIAISON AND COORDINATION OPERATIONS

4-33. Liaison teams play a key role in PSYOP mission effectiveness. When using liaison teams, commanders must use organic, uncommitted personnel. The senior PSYOP commander in the AO exchanges PSYOP liaison personnel with the supported units, U.S. nonmilitary agencies (as appropriate), and allied military organizations. The exchange of liaison personnel provides a network of proper mutual support and synchronization. PSYOP personnel at all levels must be ready to assume liaison duties.

Chapter 5

MISSION PLANNING AND TARGETING

The goal of all PSYOP planning is to create an environment that aggressively integrates PSYOP into the achievement of the supported commander's objectives. Commanders must incorporate PSYOP into all planning early in the process to ensure force integration and synchronization of activities. To remain effective, PSYOP must be constantly assessed in order to determine if modifications of the PSYOP effort are required.

PLANNING

5-1. Planning is a process. Change is a constant in war planning as assumptions are shown to be false, operations are more successful or less successful, and political events change military objectives. Even as one plan is about to be executed, planners are turning their attention to the next anticipated operation. Flexibility, adaptability, and adjustment are critical to all planning. The importance of adjusting PSYOP plans and series in response to events in the battlespace cannot be overemphasized.

5-2. PSYOP planners must be agile to be successful in an environment that has simultaneous and competing requirements to plan for an event that is in itself an ongoing process. At any given moment, PSYOP forces may be disseminating messages while military forces are executing a PSYACT in support of PSYOP objectives. At the same time, planners are readying the next action or message and evaluating the effects of the ongoing mission. Managing this dynamic and ongoing series of events is central to creating and adjusting an effective PSYOP plan. Therefore, the need for PSYOP planners to anticipate situations where PSYOP will be crucial to the military operation is essential to success.

> *Most PSYOP activities and accomplishments in Panama were hardly noticed by either the U.S. public or the general military community. But the special operations community did notice. The lessons learned in Panama were incorporated into standing operating procedures. Where possible, immediate changes were made to capitalize on the PSYOP successes of Operations JUST CAUSE and PROMOTE LIBERTY. This led to improved production, performance, and effect in the next contingency, which took place within 6 months after the return of the last PSYOP elements from Panama. Operations DESERT SHIELD and DESERT STORM employed PSYOP of an order of magnitude and effectiveness which many credit to the lessons learned from Panama.*
>
> USSOCOM Report, "Psychological Operations in Panama during Operations JUST CAUSE and PROMOTE LIBERTY," March 1994

ENVIRONMENT

5-3. U.S. law makes Service chiefs responsible for the expansion of the force to meet combatant command requirements (mobilization planning). Combatant commanders are charged with employing U.S. forces. Consequently, the CJCS and combatant commanders are primarily responsible for conducting operational planning. Employment planning occurs within the joint operational planning environment for this reason.

5-4. The national security strategy (NSS), national military strategy (NMS), Unified Command Plan (UCP), and JSCP provide guidance to the combatant commands to devise theater strategies. The combatant commands develop OPLANs and OPORDs that the joint staff reviews. Theater strategies form the basis for employment planning, drive peacetime planning, and provide a point of departure for force projection operations and general war planning. The planning that occurs to fulfill the GCC's theater security cooperation plans (formerly theater engagement plans [TEPs]) frequently eases the transition to contingency planning. The knowledge and expertise developed to support peacetime PSYOP taskings such as HMA, CD, or HA are valuable in preparing a PSYOP plan to support joint planning processes during crises and conflict.

PROCESSES

5-5. PSYOP planners will be required to conduct planning in several contexts: Army, joint, interagency, and multinational planning. They start by using the Army's military decision-making process (MDMP) to synchronize the movement and employment of military units. The MDMP also allows them to apply a rigorous analytical framework to missions of influence and persuasion. Because GCCs (combatant or force commanders) employ U.S. forces, planners use the Joint Operation Planning and Execution System (JOPES) to integrate PSYOP units with those of the joint force. This integration into joint planning may require using the deliberate or crisis action planning (CAP) process, depending upon the situation. Because PSYOP are frequently multinational, planners apply any existing President and/or SecDef guidance for multinational operations and alliance planning processes.

JOINT PLANNING OVERVIEW

5-6. Joint operation planning is coordinated through all levels of our national structure. It includes the President and/or SecDef and the joint planning and execution community (JPEC). The focus of the process is at the combatant commands, where it is used with JOPES to determine the best method of accomplishing assigned tasks and to direct the actions necessary to accomplish the mission. Joint planning includes the preparation of the following—

- OPORDs.
- OPLANs.
- Concept plans (CONPLANs).
- Functional plans.
- Campaign plans by commanders of JTFs.

5-7. Joint planning also includes those joint activities that support the development of the plans and orders listed above. This sequential process occurs simultaneously at the strategic, operational, and tactical levels of war.

5-8. Joint operation planning encompasses activities to support mobilization, deployment, employment, sustainment, and redeployment of forces. In peacetime, this application translates into deliberate plans. In conflict, joint operation planning is shortened to respond to dynamic and rapidly changing events. In wartime, joint operation planning allows for greater decentralization of joint planning activities.

5-9. Joint planning employs a system that integrates the activities of the entire JPEC through a system that provides for uniform policies, procedures, and reporting structures supported by modern communications and automated data processing. JOPES is the system that best provides standardization for the following—

- Procedures.
- Formats.
- Data files.
- Identification of shortfalls.
- Plan refinement and review.
- Rapid conversion of campaign plans and OPLANs into OPORDs for execution.

JOPES consists first and foremost of policies and procedures that guide joint operation planning efforts for U.S. personnel.

> *Mobilization and deployment of PSYOP forces were shaped by an overlapping sequence of events in the Active and Reserve Components (AC/RC). Requirements to augment the AC's 8th PSYOP Battalion and other early deployed units were identified by the planning cell acting on behalf of USCENTCOM (U.S. Central Command). The action led to deployment of the 4th PSYOP Group (AC) and to a call up of select USAR PSYOP teams.*
>
> "Psychological Operations during Operations DESERT SHIELD/STORM: A Post-Operational Analysis," USSOCOM

CAMPAIGN PLANNING

5-10. The campaign planning process represents the art of linking major operations, battles, and engagements in an operational design to accomplish theater strategic objectives. Combatant commanders translate national and theater strategy into strategic and operational concepts through the development of campaign plans. These plans represent their strategic view of related operations necessary to attain theater strategic objectives. Campaign planning can begin before or during deliberate planning, but it is not completed until after CAP, thus combining both planning processes. A campaign is the synchronization of air, land, sea, space, SO, and interagency and multinational operations in harmony with diplomatic, economic, and informational efforts to attain national objectives.

DELIBERATE AND CRISIS ACTION PLANNING

5-11. Plans are categorized and proposed under different processes, depending on the focus of a specific plan. They are labeled as deliberate planning or CAP, but both of the following are interrelated:

- Deliberate planning process is a means to develop joint OPLANs for contingencies based upon the best available information, using forces and resources allocated for deliberate planning by the JSCP. Conducted mainly in peacetime, the process relies heavily on assumptions regarding the circumstances that will exist when the plan is implemented. Deliberate planning is a highly structured, methodical, and highly coordinated process used for all contingencies and transitions to and from war.
- CAP involves a structured process following the guidelines established in JOPES. CAP is conducted for the actual commitment of allocated forces based on the needs of the situation and follows a JOPES-prescribed, six-phase development process. Developers base this type of planning on current events and time-sensitive situations.

PSYOP plan developers applied both modes of planning, deliberate and time-sensitive, to bring about effectiveness and operational flexibility. Three months of staffing eventually produced an approved PSYOP campaign plan supportive of the USCINCCENT theater strategy.

"Psychological Operations during Operations DESERT SHIELD/STORM: A Post-Operational Analysis," USSOCOM

MULTINATIONAL PLANNING

5-12. Multinational planning takes place at the national and international levels and is a complex issue. The value of peacetime coordination and exercise programs cannot be overemphasized. Coalitions are most often characterized by one or two basic structures: parallel command or lead-nation command. Theater commanders with coordination authority for multinational operations conduct the appropriate planning efforts at their level. Processes within the coalition may be developed based on the appropriate U.S. planning process (deliberate or crisis action) to meet the situation. The PSYOP planner must understand the multinational participants' capabilities to ensure they are properly integrated into the overall plan. He must also analyze and consider multinational partners' PSYOP doctrine and planning processes.

5-13. Other considerations include C2 of PSYOP forces, the national objectives of multinational participants, release of classified material, sharing intelligence, and incompatible equipment. Clearly, the most important issues are the approval authority for all series in the joint operations area (JOA) and continuity of objectives. Unity of effort is essential to ensure all PSYOP within the JOA are coordinated. Also, PSYOP can assist multinational forces with training on PSYOP planning, techniques, and procedures for the operation. When considering integrating PSYOP from other nations, PSYOP planners must ensure a clear understanding of the other nation's intent, restrictions, capabilities, political will, and national interests in the operation. When a U.S. POTF forms the core of a multinational

PSYOP effort, the rapid integration into all aspects of the PSYOP process is strongly recommended.

MEASURES OF EFFECTIVENESS

5-14. PSYOP measures of effectiveness (MOEs) provide a systematic means of assessing and reporting the impact a PSYOP program (series of PSYOP products and actions) has on specific foreign TAs. PSYOP MOEs, as all MOEs, change from mission to mission and encompass a wide range of factors that are fundamental to the overall effect of PSYOP. PSYOP impact indicators collectively provide an indication of the overall effectiveness of the PSYOP mission. Development of MOEs and their associated impact indicators (derived from measurable SPOs) must be done during the planning process. By determining the measures in the planning process, PSYOP planners ensure that organic assets and PSYOP enablers, such as intelligence, are identified to assist in evaluating MOEs for the execution of PSYOP. Evaluating the effectiveness of PSYOP may take weeks or longer given the inherent difficulties and complexity of determining cause-and-effect relationships with respect to human behavior.

MILITARY DECISION-MAKING PROCESS

5-15. Like any process, PSYOP planning has required inputs. The inputs are transformed by actions, and the process results in outputs. The process in this chapter explains how to develop an effective PSYOP plan by using the critical sources found internal and external to the unit. This process is a means to an end; the final output must be an effective, executable, and integrated PSYOP plan.

5-16. The MDMP is a single, established, and proven analytical process (Figure 5-1, page 66). It is a version of the Army's analytical approach to problem solving and is a tool that helps the commander and staff develop a plan.

SEVEN STEPS OF THE MDMP

5-17. FM 5-0, *Army Planning and Orders Production,* details the seven steps of the MDMP. What FM 5-0 does not describe in detail is the interrelationship of PSYOP planning with the MDMP. As a member of a joint or multinational staff, a member of a PSYOP group or battalion, or a liaison officer to a supported unit, the PSYOP officer plays a critical role in the MDMP. The PSYOP officer is a subject-matter expert and a member of the planning team. For a more detailed discussion on PSYOP in the MDMP, see FM 3-05.301, Chapter 4.

STEP 1: RECEIPT OF MISSION

5-18. Upon receipt of the mission, the PSYOP planner must begin gathering the tools to begin mission analysis. This step requires collecting all pertinent facts and data that may impact the mission. Essentially, the task is to assist the supported unit in the development of their plan from a PSYOP perspective.

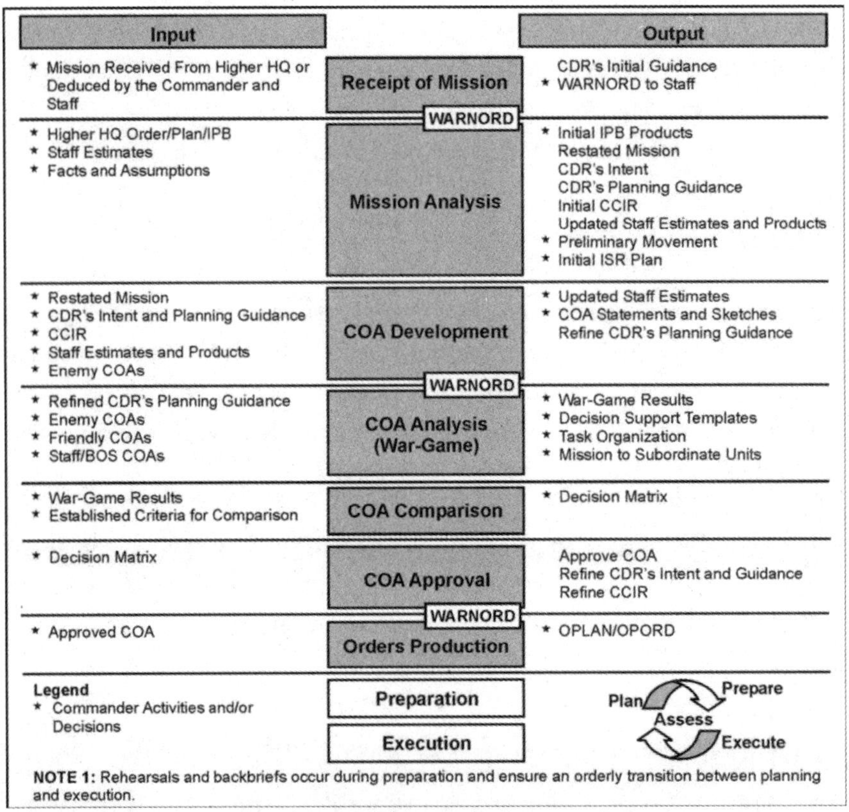

Figure 5-1. The MDMP

When consistent with prevailing cultural, political, and military realities, U.S. psychological operations were effective. Commanders particularly valued the PSYOP loudspeaker teams that promoted the peaceful surrender of enemy units and helped quiet indigenous-on-indigenous violence and other civil disturbances. However, military attacks and accompanying PSYOP appeals aimed at producing beneficial results proved counterproductive when the assumptions underlying U.S. military operations failed to reflect adequately the existing cultural, political, and military realities. Such was the case in Mogadishu with the U.S. helicopter and AC-130 gunship attacks and the U.S. and UN ground operations against Aideed's weapons caches, radio station, and headquarters sites during June and July of 1993. While mutually effective in reducing Aideed's immediate weapons inventories and neutralizing his radio, the cumulative effects of these attacks were politically and psychologically counterproductive. Designed to destroy Aideed's power base, the attacks instead increased Somalian support for Aideed and intensified Somalian opposition to U.S. and UN forces.

Arroyo Center (Rand Corporation) Report,
"Information-Related Operations
in Smaller-Scale Contingencies," 1998

STEP 2: MISSION ANALYSIS

5-19. Mission analysis consists of 17 tasks, not necessarily sequential, and results in a formal staff brief to the commander. The 17 tasks are as follows:

- Task 1: Analyze the Higher HQ Order (done by the supported unit with PSYOP assistance).
- Task 2: Conduct Initial Intelligence Preparation of the Battlespace (IPB).
- Task 3: Determine Specified, Implied, and Essential Tasks (done by the supported unit with PSYOP assistance).
- Task 4: Review Available Assets.
- Task 5: Determine Constraints.
- Task 6: Identify Critical Facts and Assumptions.
- Task 7: Conduct Risk Assessment.

- Task 8: Determine Initial Commander's Critical Information Requirement (CCIR).
- Task 9: Determine the Initial Reconnaissance Annex.
- Task 10: Plan Use of Available Time.
- Task 11: Write the Restated Mission.
- Task 12: Conduct a Mission Analysis Briefing.
- Task 13: Approve the Restated Mission.
- Task 14: Develop the Initial Commander's Intent.
- Task 15: Issue the Commander's Guidance.
- Task 16. Issue a Warning Order.
- Task 17. Review Facts and Assumptions.

5-20. PSYOP planners during this step begin the PSYOP estimate. Figure 5-2, pages 69 and 70, is the format to use when conducting a PSYOP estimate. This document can serve as a tool for the entire MDMP process and may not be able to be completed at this point, but the planners should have the regional PSYOP battalion and the SSD working on it while he is integrating into the supported unit's planning cycle. The supported unit's G-2/S-2 may be able to assist greatly in completing portions of the estimate.

5-21. Time is critical to planning and executing successful operations and must be considered an integral part of mission analysis. Many tools exist to track the external and internal flow of the battle. Associating steps with events or times of the supported commander's plan will provide an overall, broad perspective of how the mission will unfold. For example, a detailed POTF event matrix is an excellent tool to track all the events necessary to support each PSYOP program (Figures 5-3 and 5-4, pages 71 and 72). Also planners must incorporate PSYOP enabling actions into the planning and tracking process. A PSYOP enabling action is an action required of non-PSYOP units or non-DOD agencies in order to facilitate or enable execution of a PSYOP program developed to support a CJTF, GCC, or other non-DOD agency.

> *Actions such as shows of force or limited strikes may have a psychological impact, but they are not PSYOP unless the primary purpose is to influence the emotions, motives, objective reasoning, or behavior of the targeted audience.*
>
> Joint Pub 3-53

(CLASSIFICATION)

Headquarters
Place
Date, time, and zone

PSYOP ESTIMATE OF THE SITUATION NO._______

(U) REFERENCES:

a. ( ) List maps and charts.

b. ( ) Include other relevant documents (military capability study, SPSs, SPAs, and intelligence estimates).

(1) ( ) When the PSYOP estimate is distributed outside the issuing HQ, the first line of the heading is the official designation of the issuing command, and the final page of the estimate is modified to include authentication by the originating section, division, or other official, according to local policy.

(2) ( ) Normally, PSYOP estimates are numbered sequentially within a calendar year. The estimate is usually distributed as an appendix to the operations annex.

1. ( ) MISSION.

a. ( ) Supported unit's restated mission resulting from mission analysis.

b. ( ) PSYOP mission statement. Describe the PSYOP mission to support the maneuver commander's mission. This should be in the format of PSYOP supports XXXXXX (supported unit) by Psychological Operations objective (PO), PO, PO, PO, and PO.

2. ( ) SITUATION AND CONSIDERATION.

a. ( ) Characteristics of the AO.

(1) ( ) Weather. How will weather affect the dissemination of PSYOP products and access to TAs? (Winds–leaflet drops, precipitation–print products, etc.) End Product–PSYOP Weather Overlay.

(2) ( ) Terrain. How will terrain affect dissemination of PSYOP products and movement of tactical PSYOP elements? End Product–PSYOP Terrain Overlay.

(3) ( ) Analysis of media infrastructure. (Location and broadcast range of radio and TV broadcast facilities, retransmission towers, print facilities, distribution and dissemination nodes; identification of denied areas [not accessible by particular medium].) End Product–PSYOP Media Infrastructure Overlay.

b. ( ) Key target sets. (**Note:** These sets will be further refined into a PTAL. The TAs will then be analyzed and further refined during the TAA process.) (Reason: FM 5-0 labels this section "Enemy Forces." This is not the only target set that PSYOP personnel will have to deal with. To fully support the supported unit commander, PSYOP personnel must consider all key target sets, not solely enemy forces.) PSYOP key target sets overlays (hostile, friendly, neutral) include the following:

(1) ( ) Hostile target sets. For each hostile target set, identify strength, disposition, composition, capabilities (ability to conduct propaganda, ability to help or hinder the PSYOP effort), and probable COAs as they relate to PSYOP.

(2) ( ) Friendly target sets. For each friendly target set, identify strength, disposition, composition, capabilities (ability to conduct propaganda, ability to help or hinder the PSYOP effort), and probable COAs as they relate to PSYOP.

(3) ( ) Neutral target sets. (Include target sets whose attitudes are unknown.) For each neutral target set, identify strength, disposition, composition, capabilities (ability to conduct propaganda, ability to help or hinder the PSYOP effort), and probable COAs as they relate to PSYOP.

c. ( ) Friendly forces.

(1) ( ) Supported unit COAs. State the COAs under consideration and the PSYOP-specific requirements needed to support each COA.

(CLASSIFICATION)

(CLASSIFICATION)

(2) ( ) Current status of organic personnel and resources. State availability of organic personnel and resources needed to support each COA under consideration. Consider PSYOP-specific personnel, other MOSs and availability of PSYOP-specific equipment.
(3) ( ) Current status of nonorganic personnel and resources. State availability of nonorganic resources needed to support each COA. Consider linguistic support, COMMANDO SOLO, leaflet-dropping aircraft, and RC PSYOP forces.
(4) ( ) Comparison of requirements versus capabilities and recommended solutions. Compare PSYOP requirements for each COA with current PSYOP capabilities. List recommended solutions for any shortfall in capabilities.
(5) ( ) Key considerations (evaluation criteria) for COA supportability. List evaluation criteria to be used in COA analysis and COA comparison.

d. ( ) Assumptions. State assumptions about the PSYOP situation made for this estimate. (For example, Assumption: Enemy propaganda broadcast facilities will be destroyed by friendly forces not later than (NLT) D+2.)

3. ( ) ANALYSIS OF COAs.

a. ( ) Analyze each COA from the PSYOP point of view to determine its advantages and disadvantages for conducting PSYOP. The level of command, scope of contemplated operations, and urgency of need determine the detail in which the analysis is made.

b. ( ) The evaluation criteria listed in paragraph 2.c.(5) above establish the elements to be analyzed for each COA under consideration. Examine these factors realistically and include appropriate considerations that may have an impact on the PSYOP situation as it affects the COAs. (Throughout the analysis, the staff officer must keep PSYOP considerations foremost in his mind. The analysis is not intended to produce a decision, but to ensure that all applicable PSYOP factors have been considered and are the basis of paragraphs 4 and 5.)

4. ( ) COMPARISON OF COAs.

a. ( ) Compare the proposed COAs to determine the one that offers the best chance of success from the PSYOP point of view. List the advantages and disadvantages of each COA affecting PSYOP. Comparison should be visually supported by a decision matrix.

b. ( ) Develop and compare methods of overcoming disadvantages, if any, in each COA.

c. ( ) State a general conclusion on the COA that offers the best chance of success from a PSYOP perspective.

5. ( ) RECOMMENDATIONS AND CONCLUSIONS.

a. ( ) Recommended COA based on comparison (most supportable from the PSYOP perspective). Rank COAs from best to worst.

b. ( ) Issues, deficiencies, and risks for each COA, with recommendations to reduce their impact.

(signed) ____________________
G-3/G-7 PSYOP Officer
ANNEXES:
DISTRIBUTION:

(CLASSIFICATION)

Figure 5-2. PSYOP Estimate of the Situation

STEP 3: COURSE OF ACTION DEVELOPMENT

5-22. Because PSYOP are a unique combat multiplier, there are many methods to engage the TA. PSYOP participate in the full range of operations from peacetime missions, to a regional escalation and perhaps war, through postconflict termination, and the return to a peacetime profile. PSYOP support to courses of action (COAs) may vary due to differences in employment of the main effort, task-organization, TA, objectives, the use and composition of forces, and the scheme of maneuver (or the footprint for dissemination by PSYOP).

Phase	I	II	III	IV	V
	Predeployment	**Deployment/Combat Operations**	**Hostilities**	**Transition Operations**	**Civil-Military Operations**
Decision Point	• Approve Allocation of Air • Short Notice NEO • WX Confirmation	• Transition COMJSOTF • Revalidate Assumptions • Objectives/Conditions Achieved	• Delay Relief in Place • Establish Interim Police • Receive Coalition OPS • Begin Relief OPS • Begin Transition OPS	• Reduce or Eliminate CAS • Install GOV Officials • Begin Redeployment of Selected Units	
Day	D-2 D-1	D+1 D+2	D+3 D+6	D+7 D+8 D+9	D+10 D+14
JPOTF	• Preposition TMPC • Nominate TGTs to JFACC • Acquire HN Broadcast Facilities • Complete External Information Plan	• Execute Strategic, Operational and Tactical PSYOP Plan (TV, Radio, Print, Loud Speaker, Operations)	See Figure 5-4, page 5-12	• Support CMO Plan • Assist in the Introduction of Stabilization Forces • Complete POAT for Phase V	• Integrate PSYOP Forces Into CMO Plan • Complete Redeployment • Transition Plan
ARFOR	• H-53 AVN Deploys to ISB • H-48 AVN Arrives ISB	• Detainee Facility OPNL • Initial CMO Assessment Complete • JSOTF/ARFOR Handover Complete	• D+3 Man Checkpoints • Secure Key Facilities • Assist NGOs/OGAs as Required • Final CMO Assessment Complete	• Chop Selected Forces to the JTF • CS/CSS Transition OPs	• Conduct CMO in AO • Continue to Secure Key Facilities • Maintain Civil Order • Maintain JTF Reserve • Provide CSS to JSOTF
JSOTF (MANEUVER)	• Stand UP HQ	• TF Insertions Continue • CMO Assessment Complete • JSOTF/ARFOR Handover Complete	• Assist NGOs/OGAs as Required • Transition Coordination with JTF/MNF • CA, PSYOP Linguists Transition to JTF	• Expand CMO to outlying areas • Support Permanent Stabilization • Complete Redeployment of Selected Forces. • Chop Selected Forces to JTF/MNF	• Expand FID • Maintain Civil Order • Be Prepared to Assist in NEO • Prepare to Redeploy
AFFOR	• Transmit ATO/ACO • KC-135 Arrives JOA	• Airlift/AEROMEDEVAC	• Terminate ATO/Peacetime Flight Plan • JFACC A/C Redeployment • Final Transition Coordination	• Chop Selected Forces to JTF/MNF	• Provide Airlift and AEROMEDEVAC • Operate and Maintain HN Airports • Be Prepared to Assist NEO
NAVFOR	• SAR Ship/AC in Position • Complete Adv Force Tgting	• ARFOR/MARFOR Link-Up • Detainee Facility EST • MARFOR Security OPS	• Transition JRCC Function on Shore • MARFOR Prepare for W/D and handover to F/O Forces	• Begin Relief Operations	• Conduct CMI in AO • Be Prepared to Redeploy
Intel		• Locate Insurgent Nodes • ID/Locate Insurgent Leadership • BDA on Tag/OBJs	• ID Threat to JTF Deployment and Relief Operations • ID Criminal Organizations Targeting U.S. Forces and Assets	• ID Terrorists Threats to Redeploying Forces • Set Transitions	
Fires		• CAS/EW on Call	• Maintain CAS on Strip Alert	• Force Protection	
C4I2	• EC 135s Propositioned • COMMEX	• JTF Forward Operational • ID/Key Required	• ID C2 Site Requirements • ID Select Units for Redeployment • Finalize Coalition Force AO's and Command Relationships	• Transition Phase IV EST Coalition HQ • Assign Coalition Force AOs and Command Relationships	
JTF	• Rehearsals	• 2d BCT Prepared to Deploy • LNO's 1 and 2 BCT Deploy • JTF Reserve Deploys	• Begin Initial Relief Operations	• Follow on JTF/MNF to assume JOA	• Execute Transition With Follow on JTF

Figure 5-3. Example of PSYOP Synchronization Matrix

The stroke of genius that turns the fate of a battle? I don't believe in it. A battle is a complicated operation that you prepare laboriously. If the enemy does this, you say to yourself I will do that. If such and such happens, these are the steps I shall take to meet it. You think out every possible development and decide on the way to deal with the situation created. One of these developments occurs; you put your plan in operation, and everyone says "What genius..." whereas the credit is really due to the labor of preparation.

Ferdinand Foch, Interview, April 1919

5-23. When analyzing the main effort, consider the level of PSYOP required to accomplish the commander's objectives:

- Strategic.
- Operational.
- Tactical.

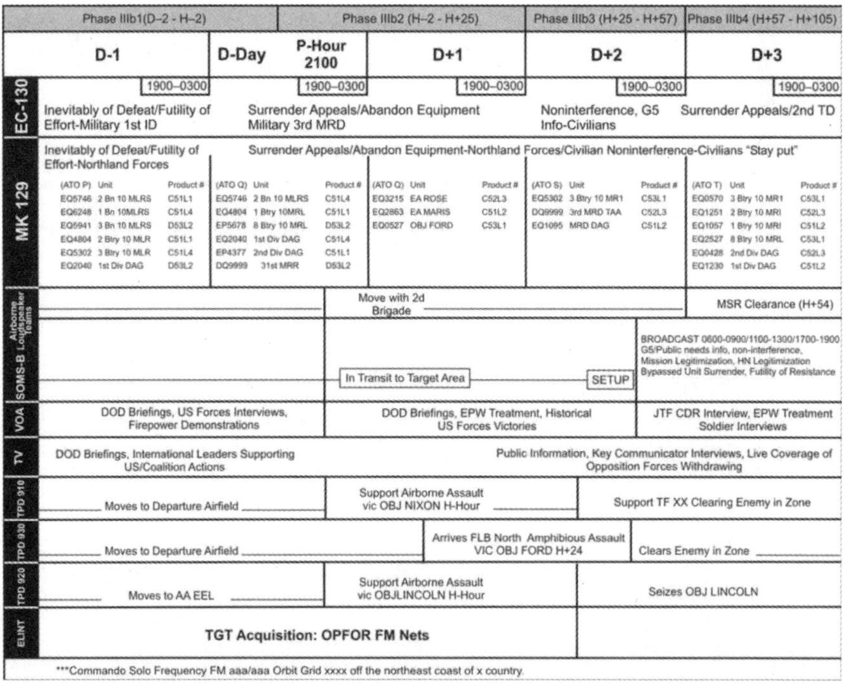

Figure 5-4. Example of Detailed Portion From Matrix

5-24. Each level may require different and unique assets as well as preparation time. Important factors driving the configuration of a POTF are the material system capabilities available. If the combatant commander requires PSYOP forces to deploy with their print and broadcast capabilities with little, if any, support from HN government or commercial infrastructure, this COA will be unique. The availability of strategic airlift to deploy organic equipment will undoubtedly impact each COA. Applying the concept of economy of force shapes the eventual structure of the main effort and the minimum forces required to accomplish the objectives for the supported commander. However, the main effort may be objective-oriented, geographically oriented, TA-oriented, or supported-unit-oriented. It could also be a mix of all of the above.

5-25. When taking into account task-organization, it is imperative to determine the size of the forward element, the rear element, and how these forces will interact. Reachback may allow for a smaller development and production force forward if the AOR and the forward elements are adequately equipped. Additionally, reachback demands increased distribution forces but dissemination and tactical forces may also require augmentation. The planner must determine the scope of the initial and follow-on forces. The task-organization may consist of Active Army, RC, or other Army components, departing and arriving from several different locations. This scenario is considered worst-case and should be avoided. The planner should attempt to maintain unit integrity whenever possible and set aside time for building the force in CONUS before an operation. The use of indigenous support, both material and labor, has a noticeable impact on reducing U.S. personnel and strategic lift requirements. However, access to foreign nationals may in some cases be restricted. Also, PSYOP forces are unique and limited in number. Rarely will a supported GCC allow his only regional PSYOP battalion to remain fully engaged in a JOA when those forces could be used somewhere else in the theater in support of other contingencies.

5-26. In addition to tailoring the force size to accomplish the mission, the TA and the objectives and supporting objectives are identified during the development of COAs. Chapter 4 discusses the configurations in which a POTF may deploy in support of a CJTF or GCC.

5-27. Unique task-organization PSE may be a consideration for peacekeeping operations or contingency operations with an extended period of transition to peace. These operations will likely require a sustained presence of PSYOP personnel to ensure that the GCC's objectives for transition operations are met. Now, more than ever, the RC plays a crucial role in operations that evolve into a long-term presence. The use of PSYOP reserve units is likely from the crisis-planning step through decisive combat operation and well into the transition to peace. Each step will likely undergo change as the introduction of RC change. The method, size, and type of PSYOP RC incorporated into the mission will necessitate unique planning considerations. Therefore, deciding when the reserves integrate into an operation will also influence, directly or indirectly, each COA.

5-28. The method of employment and how the force will deploy to the AO is the PSYOP scheme of maneuver. The PSYOP element can vary in size, scope, and mission profile, thereby impacting or shaping COAs. For example, during predeployment, a Psychological Operations assessment team (POAT) may deploy upon receipt of a deployment order to augment the J-3 PSYOP staff officer. During this step, the POTF (rear) (in garrison) may do the bulk of the product development, heavy printing, and audio or video production. Tactical PSYOP forces and I/R forces may link up with supported maneuver elements to advise and plan for deployment. Liaison officers (LNOs) will likely deploy to support the air component commander (ACC) and the JSOTF to ensure PSYOP integrates into peculiar air platforms for dissemination.

5-29. During the deployment step, the POAT may deploy to the intermediate staging base (ISB) and later be absorbed by the POTF (forward). The POTF (forward) deploys with light print, television, and radio broadcast capabilities, while the POTF (rear) may conduct all other operations from the home station. Once the POTF (forward) is established in the AOR, JOA, or the HN, the POTF (rear) may assume a supporting role or continue to serve as the primary source of PSYOP. Tactical PSYOP forces deploy into theater with supported elements or they may deploy independently and link-up with the supported unit already in-theater.

5-30. Employing the forces may include the tactical forces moving with the supported maneuver elements to conduct combat operations. If required and as lift becomes available, the POTF (rear) may deploy in phases to the JOA, AOR, or HN to more responsively support the CJTF without interrupting ongoing development and production.

NOTE: Although this example is only one scenario or scheme of maneuver for PSYOP forces, the number of variations is endless when any portion of the redeployment, deployment, or employment package undergoes a revision to suit the mission needs. As a result, entire COAs will look different when the scheme of maneuver turns to meet the objectives of the supported commander.

STEP 4: COURSE OF ACTION ANALYSIS

5-31. COA analysis consists of a feasibility check, war gaming, risk assessment, and evaluation of war-game results. The war game of the COA is critical for the commander and staff to ensure all elements including PSYOP are fully integrated and synchronized. An early decision to limit the number of COAs war-gamed, or to develop only one COA, saves the greatest amount of time in this process. Prior to the war game, PSYOP planners select criteria by which to evaluate the results of the war-gaming of each COA. An example of these criteria may be the positive or negative effects of operations on the local populace or TAs. Alternative COAs are evaluated after the war game based on how well they meet these same criteria, thereby driving a staff recommendation. Each COA must be suitable, feasible, acceptable, distinguishable, and complete.

STEP 5: COURSE OF ACTION COMPARISON

5-32. After each COA is war-gamed and it is determined that it meets the established criteria, it is compared to the other COAs. Each staff member will evaluate the advantages and disadvantages of the COAs from their perspective. The PSYOP planner will evaluate each COA to determine which will best utilize PSYOP assets, provide flexibility for contingencies, and has the highest probability of achieving mission success from the PSYOP viewpoint.

STEP 6: COURSE OF ACTION APPROVAL

5-33. The COAs are then briefed to the commander along with the staff's recommendation. The commander makes the final decision. Once the decision is made, and the commander gives any final guidance, the staff immediately issues an updated warning order (WARNO), refines the COA, and completes the plan.

STEP 7: ORDERS PRODUCTION

5-34. The PSYOP section to the base plan must ensure, regardless of the selected COA, that the following additional information is included:

- Media analysis.
- PTAL.
- PO/SPO.
- Approval process procedures.
- PSYOP support request procedures.
- Anticipated propaganda programs.
- PSYOP MOEs/IRs.

PLANNING IN A TIME-CONSTRAINED ENVIRONMENT

5-35. The focus of any planning process is to quickly develop a flexible, fully integrated, synchronized, and tactically sound plan that enhances mission success with the fewest casualties possible. Although the task is difficult, commanders must oftentimes abbreviate the planning process by cutting time. FM 5-0 states that there are several general time-saving techniques that may be used to speed up the planning process. These techniques include—

- Maximize parallel planning. Although parallel planning is the norm, maximizing its use in time-constrained environments is critical. In a time-constrained environment, the importance of WARNOs increases as available time decreases. A verbal WARNO now followed by a written order later saves more time than a written order 1 hour from now. The same WARNOs used in the full MDMP should be issued when abbreviating the process. In addition to WARNOs, units must share all available information with subordinates, especially IPB products, as early as possible. The staff uses every opportunity to perform parallel planning with the higher headquarters and to share information with subordinates. (FM 5-0, Chapter 1, further explains this topic.)

- Increase collaborative planning. Planning in real time with higher headquarters and subordinates improves the overall planning effort of the organization (FM 5-0, Chapter 1, further explains). Modern information systems (INFOSYS) and a common operational picture (COP) shared electronically allow collaboration with subordinates from distant locations and can increase information sharing and improve the commander's visualization. Additionally, taking advantage of subordinate input and their knowledge of the situation in their AO often results in developing better COAs faster.
- Use LNOs. LNOs posted to higher headquarters allow the command to have representation in their higher headquarters planning secession. LNOs assist in passing timely information to their parent headquarters and can speed up the planning effort both for the higher and own headquarters.
- Increase commander's involvement. While commanders can not spend all their time with the planning staff, the greater the commander's involvement in planning, the faster the staff can plan. In time-constrained conditions, commanders who participate in the planning process can make decisions (such as COA selection), without waiting for a detailed briefing from the staff. The first timesaving technique is to increase the commander's involvement. This technique allows commanders to make decisions during the MDMP without waiting for detailed briefings after each step.
- Limit the number of COAs to develop. Limiting the number of COAs developed and wargamed can save a large amount of planning time. If time is extremely short, the commander can direct development of only one COA. In this case, the goal is an acceptable COA that meets mission requirements in the time available, even if the COA is not optimal. This technique saves the most time.

5-36. In all instances, however, when the PSYOP planner abbreviates the planning process, the initial guidance must—

- Specify the organization's essential tasks.
- Approve the unit's restated mission.
- Issue a WARNO.

PSYOP IN THE TARGETING PROCESS

5-37. Targeting is the process of selecting targets and matching the appropriate response to them, taking into account operational requirements and force capabilities. Targeting is intended to delay, disrupt, divert, or destroy the adversary's military potential throughout the depth of the operational area. Military influence, via information or violent action, is brought to bear on the opponent's own military and economic infrastructure. Communications capabilities at the operational and tactical levels are the means to this end. To maintain a common frame of reference, PSYOP planners must use the same terminology used by the other planners with whom they work.

5-38. MOEs are closely tied to targeting. PSYOP MOEs, as all MOEs, change from mission to mission and are critical to the PSYOP process. By determining them in the planning process, the PSYOP planner ensures assets are identified to execute effects assessment both during and following the operation.

5-39. It is essential that PSYOP planning and targeting be performed concurrently with the development of the higher HQ CONPLAN or OPLAN. PSYOP planning and targeting is merely a component of the MDMP; the PSYOP officer must plan in concert with the entire combined arms battle staff. As a component commander within a JTF or as a member of a battle staff, the PSYOP officer contributes to each step (or task) of the MDMP and gains needed information to make decisions while formulating and refining the PSYOP plan.

NOTE: Just as in indirect fire planning, PSYOP must be truly integrated into the targeting process and its functions of decide, detect, deliver, and assess.

5-40. Targeting and MDMP are closely related, but where and how they are integrated or related is not always clear. PSYOP targeting must help the battle staff to integrate the targeting functions into the existing MDMP and must reflect the results of the targeting process (Figure 5-5, below). The requirements of the PSYOP targeting process at the unified or JTF level and below must be achieved within the MDMP and must be achieved without separate processes or additional sets of steps (or tasks). If targeting is successfully integrated into the MDMP, the PSYOP targeting plan will likely answer the following questions:

- What specific target audiences, nodes, or links must we attack and what objectives must we achieve with specific PSYOP assets to support the commander's intent and the concept of the operation? *(Decide)*
- What resources are necessary to analyze conditions, vulnerabilities, susceptibilities, and accessibility to change the behavior of the desired TAs? How do we develop and design series to change the behavior of selected TAs? *(Detect)*
- How and when a series is executed (production, distribution, and dissemination)? *(Deliver)*
- How do we determine the degree to which we have achieved our SPO? *(Assess)*

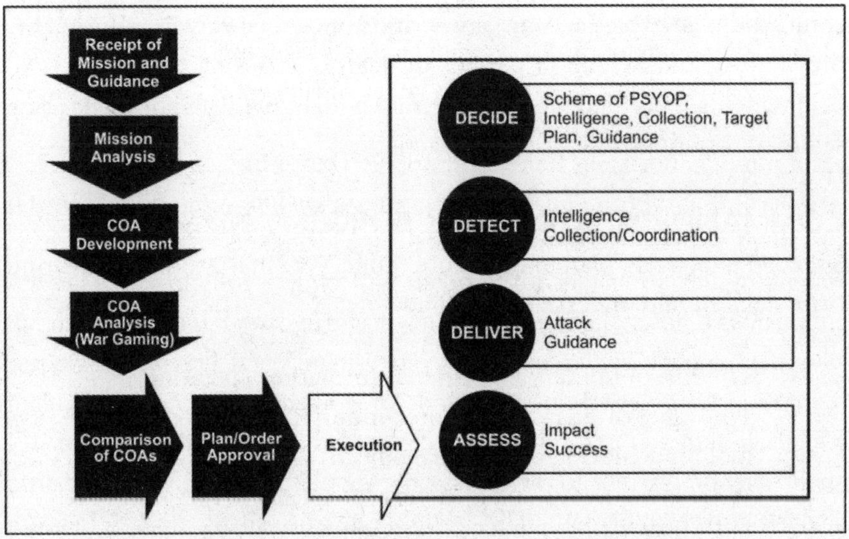

Figure 5-5. Targeting Plan Integrated into the MDMP

5-41. The key to all PSYOP is to ensure that the series are directed at TAs who possess the ability to accomplish the action targeted behavior. Key decision makers are individuals who may have the ability to achieve a U.S. national or military objective. They are natural targets of U.S. influence involving the use of one or more elements of national power, to include the military and informational pillars of national power. Although key decision makers are one avenue to pursue in reaching the commander's objectives, many other audiences are equally as important. The analysis usually boils down to these questions: What behaviors do we need to change? Who can change them? How do we get the TA to change their behavior?

5-42. PSYOP span the range of military operations. Specific planning options and sequencing of events guide PSYOP activities during each operation. Changes in political objectives or constraints may cause operational characteristics to change rapidly and significantly. Experience has repeatedly demonstrated that it is essential to include PSYOP planning from the start, and that those who will execute the mission must be involved in the planning process.

TRAINING

5-43. Commanders should ensure that their staffs and units are resourced and receive training in planning PSYOP. Staff training can occur during command post exercises, war games, and conceptual exercises during the preparatory and execution periods of field exercises or routine forward deployments. Commanders can also train both individuals and staffs using seminars, briefings, and other such activities.

COMMANDERS, JOINT TASK FORCES, AND STAFFS

5-44. To effectively plan and execute military PSYOP, commanders and their staffs should understand the following:

- The role of military PSYOP in information operations.
- The value of PSYOP as a force multiplier and as a cost-effective tool for achieving operational objectives.
- What is required to plan and execute effective PSYOP.
- Polices that govern the use of PSYOP.

5-45. Those assigned as operational planners should understand the following:

- The process for addressing military PSYOP during the preparation of staff and commander's estimates and the origination of COAs.
- The broad range of what can and cannot be reasonably executed as PSYOP.
- How the other information operations capabilities and related activities support PSYOP.

PSYOP PLANNERS

5-46. The selection and training of PSYOP planners is critical. It is essential that military PSYOP planners possess the ability to "think outside the box," because the ability to create and execute an effective PSYOP plan consisting of both products and actions depends upon the creativity used to develop and maintain a program. PSYOP planners must possess the following abilities:

- Understand each component's PSYOP and IO capabilities.
- Be intimately familiar with their command's assigned missions and operational area.
- Understand the concepts of centers of gravity, initiative, security, and surprise.
- Understand the psychological and cultural factors that might influence the adversary's planning and decision making.
- Understand potential adversaries' planning and decision-making processes (both formal and informal).
- Understand the specialized devices and weapons systems that are available to support PSYOP.
- Understand how the PSYOP process integrates into the MDMP.

SPECIFIC PLANNING CONSIDERATIONS

5-47. There are several areas that should be considered when planning for PSYOP. These range from the strategic to operational to tactical levels and reflect the breadth of activity that impact on and are affected by PSYOP. Four areas to consider are—

- *Planning.*
  - Determine the national and military strategies and U.S. national security policy for the region.
  - Consider potential missions or tasks from the President and/or SecDef or GCC.
  - Understand how the PSYOP process integrates into the MDMP.
  - Review the already-approved PSYOP themes and objectives contained in the JSCP.
  - "Plug-in" to the supported commander's information operations cell (IOC).
  - Ensure the command relationship is clear within the JTF and the supporting units.
  - Locate and plan for sufficient contracting officers with appropriate authority.
  - Consider and plan for early conduct of military PSYOP and, if required, use HN resources and non-PSYOP military assets for media production and dissemination; for example, use of naval ship printing facilities for production of PSYOP products.
  - Analyze the current ROE.
  - Ensure the COA is consistent with the law of armed conflict.
  - Define any treaty or legal obligations the United States may have with the region or country that might enhance or constrain the mission.
  - Determine precisely what must be accomplished in the operation to strengthen or support the objectives established by the GCC.
  - Plan the movement of major end items.
  - Ensure comprehensive coordination of plans, with an emphasis on those staff elements or agencies that generate information, such as public affairs, so all information operations activities are concordant.

- *Agencies.*
  - Establish a relationship with the following agencies or commands as necessary: Joint Information Operations Center (JIOC), Joint Spectrum Center (JSC), Human Factors Analysis Center (HFAC), 1st IOC, naval information warfare agency (NIWA), Air Force Information Warfare Center (AFIWC), Joint Warfare Analysis Center (JWAC), and the Joint Communications Support Element (JCSE). Inform these agencies of your need for specialized support in the future.
  - Establish a link with the Joint Intelligence Center (JIC).
  - Establish a liaison with the joint communications center.

- *IPB.*
  - Select the type of PSYOP that are most advantageous for the current situation.
  - Monitor adversary situation and how changes may impact the current COAs.
  - Identify and select key friendly, adversary, and neutral TAs.
  - Analyze the current operations security and military deception measures that have been planned. Integrate these into the PSYOP plan.
  - Analyze foreign governments' attitudes and reactions toward military capabilities and U.S. intentions.
  - Appraise the level of opposition that can be expected from hostile governments.
  - Determine what support can be expected from friendly and allied coalition governments.
  - Determine the key personnel within the media pool, if appropriate.
  - Consider the effects of terrain, weather, and nuclear, biological, and chemical (NBC) environment on forces and equipment, and the planned method for dissemination of PSYOP products.

  - Define the current situation (who, what, where, when, and why).
  - Review the supported commander's intelligence collection plan as a reference for PSYOP information.

- *Communication.*
  - Ensure all LNO requirements have been met.
  - Confirm frequency deconfliction.
  - Verify the joint communications-electronics operation instructions are adequate.
  - Determine if there is a need for joint airborne communications assets.
  - Ensure all special command and control communications, to include computer systems, have global capabilities and can communicate with the entire JTF.

ESSENTIAL PLANNING DOCUMENTS

5-48. Planning documents, such as tabs, appendixes, annexes and orders are essential to the conduct of any operation. When accurately done, these documents detail how an operation is to be conducted and what the end states are.

EXTERNAL INFORMATION PLAN

5-49. An external information plan must be coordinated with the International Public Information Committee (IPIC) through the CJCS-J39IO and the ASD(SO/LIC). This plan constitutes a request for support and aids synergy. It is not an order. The external information plan should contain the following as a minimum:

- Recommended objectives, themes, actions, and timings requested for interagency consideration and implementation.
- Requested support from key communicators.
- Requested co-use of facilities, equipment, and informational materials.
- Requested authority for use of U.S. international media programming.

PSYOP Tab of the Information Operations Appendix to the Supported Commander's Plan

5-50. The PSYOP tab of the information operations appendix to the supported commander's plan is prepared for the supported GCC and JTF commanders. Further plans at the tactical level may be prepared and tailored to the needs of Service component, functional component, and other tactical-level commanders using these plans as a guide. Changes, additions, or deletions to the PSYOP portion of GCC and JTF plans are not recognized for action unless coordinated and approved by the PSYOP commander.

5-51. The overall PSYOP planning effort should include the PSYOP tab/appendix section of the supported commanders' plan. This section will include summarized intelligence, task-organization, PSYOP mission, concept of operations, coordinating instructions, Service support information, product and program approval authorities, POs and SPOs, PTAL, themes to be stressed and avoided, media to be used, constraints and limitations for PSYOP forces, an external synchronization matrix, and a proposed lethal and nonlethal target list.

Military Plans and Orders

5-52. Military plans and orders should be prepared by PSYOP planners to direct and coordinate operations of PSYOP forces and input to the plans and orders of others to ensure synchronization and support. The PSYOP support plan for the PSE or POTF, as a minimum, should include the situation, mission, task-organization, commander's intent, concept of operations (CONOPS), scheme of maneuver, subordinate unit missions, coordinating instructions, administration and logistics, and command and signal information. It also includes the following annexes:

- Annex A – Task Organization, to include location.
- Annex B – Intelligence.
    - TAAWs.
    - Supporting Psychological Operations assessment (SPA), special Psychological Operations study (SPS).
    - Priority intelligence requirements (PIR)/intelligence requirements.

- Enemy disposition.
- Anticipated opponent PSYOP and information plan.
- Population status.
- Media infrastructure.
- Language analysis.
- Religion analysis.
- Ethnic group analysis.
- Weather analysis.
- Terrain impact on dissemination.
- Reconnaissance and surveillance plan.
- Area study.
- Architecture of connectivity.

- Annex C – Operations.
  - PSYOP programs and supporting PSYOP programs.
  - Dissemination means.
  - PSYOP situation report (SITREP) format.
  - Approval process.
  - Reachback process.

- Annex D – Logistics.
  - Logistical support.
  - Request for PSYOP support format.
  - POTF or PSE statement of requirement (SOR).
  - Logistic purchase request.
  - PSYOP-specific support.
  - SOF (SOTSE) support.

- Annex E – Signal.
  - Communication security.
  - Bandwidth requirements.
  - Joint frequency management.
  - Transmission system.
  - Data network communication.
  - Information assurance.
  - Communication network management.
  - Coalition communication.

Chapter 6

EMPLOYMENT

PSYOP forces conduct the PSYOP process in support of operations approved by the President and/or SecDef, combatant commanders, U.S. Country Teams, OGAs, and multinational forces across the range of military operations from peace through conflict to war. Like all ARSOF, PSYOP units participate in operations that have a variety of profiles and complex requirements. After applying the Army SO imperatives and the MDMP to a particular mission, PSYOP commanders bring all their resources to bear by tailoring the force to meet unique administrative and operational requirements.

Mission analysis determines the need for the establishment of either a POTF or PSE. The POTF is the foundation for operations that have large PSYOP requirements. The POTF ensures that all missions that have a psychological effect on the adversary are planned, coordinated, and executed. The POTF ensures that the appropriate mix of regional, tactical, and dissemination capabilities are employed. A PSE is used for smaller-scale operations but has the same responsibility of ensuring that appropriate capabilities are employed to successfully complete the mission. The PSE is a smaller force without the robust C2 that is inherent in a POTF. This chapter examines task-organized PSYOP organizations tailored to meet the supported commander's requirements for various mission profiles.

PSYCHOLOGICAL OPERATIONS PROCESS

6-1. The PSYOP process consists of seven phases (Figure 6-1, page 88) that begins with planning and ends with evaluation. The process, however, is continuous as changes are made to different series as a result of the evaluation phase. Although the process is sequential in nature it must be remembered that multiple series may be in different phases at congruent times. The PSYOP process is focused on changing behavior of foreign TAs through the execution of multiple series of PSYOP products and actions.

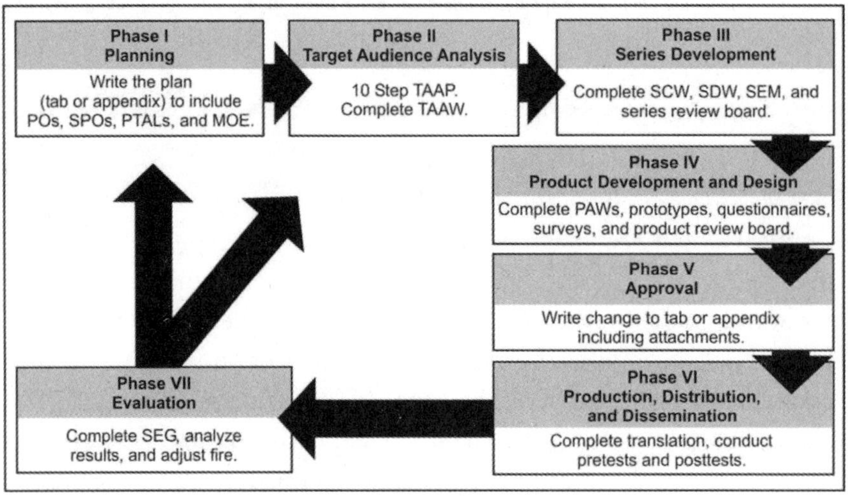

Figure 6-1. The PSYOP Process

PHASE I: PLANNING

6-2. In Phase I, POs, SPOs, potential target audiences (PTAs), and MOEs are determined. A staff planner normally conducts this phase as part of the MDMP, and often with the assistance of the POAT. During this first phase, planners formulate the POs for the supported commander's mission. POs are generally determined by the highest-level PSYOP element involved in the operation, and provide the framework for the development of the PSYOP plan. Upon approval of the POs by the SecDef, the SPOs are developed and the PTAs are identified. PSYOP MOEs establish a metric for evaluating PSYOP and are determined in a deliberative and methodical process in Phase I. Accurately assessing the effectiveness of PSYOP requires well-conceived MOEs, and the identification and early integration of organic assets and PSYOP enablers, such as intelligence, to satisfy the MOEs.

PHASE II: TARGET AUDIENCE ANALYSIS

6-3. TAA is the process by which the PTAs are refined and analyzed. Ideal TAs for PSYOP are homogenous groups that share similar conditions and vulnerabilities (needs, wants, or desires). The TAAW is the document that captures this analysis. Multiple TAAWs are generated during this phase, as all TAs under each SPO must be analyzed.

PHASE III: SERIES DEVELOPMENT

6-4. This phase entails the development of a PSYOP series, which is a completed plan conceptualized and developed to change a behavior of a TA. Specifically a PSYOP series consists of all the PSYOP products and actions designed to accomplish one behavioral change by a single TA. Since each SPO normally has multiple TAs, there is a need to develop multiple series. The source document for series development is the TAAW that was completed during Phase II of the PSYOP process. During series development, a series concept work sheet (SCW), a series dissemination work sheet (SDW), and a series execution matrix (SEM) are created.

PHASE IV: PRODUCT DEVELOPMENT AND DESIGN

6-5. Product development and design is the process of taking the product requirements, identified in series development (Phase III), and transforming them into product prototypes or planned actions. It is critical that all product prototypes in the series are completed and reviewed as a package. Since it is not always practical to produce actual product prototypes (TV spots or radio shows) for approval, the supporting PSYOP unit produces scripts, storyboards, or concept sketches as a substitute for product prototypes. During this stage, pretesting and posttesting methodologies are determined and the supporting testing instruments (surveys, questionnaires, criteria, and instructions) are developed.

PHASE V: APPROVAL

6-6. The process to obtain approval to execute the series is conducted during Phase V of the PSYOP process. The PSYOP products in the series must be approved prior to execution. Essentially, to initiate the approval process, the PSYOP element submits an executive summary, and provides the input to a fragmentary order (FRAGO) to the supported organization's OPORD for the execution of the series. The PSYOP input to the FRAGO is often written as a change to the PSYOP tab or appendix, and outlines the details for the successful conduct of PSYOP, including the support requirements for the supported unit. The modification to the PSYOP tab or appendix is submitted through the supported unit's staff for review. Upon completion of the staff's review, the series is submitted with comments to the approval authority. A streamlined staffing process ensures that the series is responsive. A protracted approval process is often the single greatest factor that prevents PSYOP from being responsive. Establishing a concurrent staffing format as opposed to a sequential one, and selecting only key staff elements to participate in the review process, significantly reduces the length of time it takes to obtain the final approval.

PHASE VI: PRODUCTION, DISTRIBUTION, AND DISSEMINATION

6-7. Upon gaining approval for a PSYOP series, the products are translated, pretested, modified according to the results, and produced. PSYOP forces have organic visual, audio, audiovisual production assets. PSYOP units below the POTF level (for example, the TPDD) may have limited production capability, such as the DPPC and the Deployable Audio Production Suite (DAPS). PSYOP forces also use nonorganic production assets and facilities (other Services, local facilities, and OGAs). Contracting with a local company during military operations is cost-effective and allows for timely and responsive production of PSYOP products. The completed products are then distributed, electronically or physically, from the production centers to the disseminators. Products can be delivered by air from CONUS to the theater of operations or transported using the supported unit's existing logistic network. The products are then disseminated to the TA using a variety of dissemination methods depending upon the type of product: audio, visual, or audiovisual. Posttesting of the products may also occur during dissemination.

PHASE VII: EVALUATION

6-8. Evaluation has two interrelated activities: testing (both pretesting and posttesting), which typically involves individual products, and ascertaining the effectiveness of the PSYOP effort over time. The latter is accomplished by analyzing impact indicators (answers to MOE or spontaneous events related to the PSYOP efforts) and determining to what extent the SPO and ultimately the PO were accomplished. Other important facets of the evaluation process occur throughout the other phases of the PSYOP process. For example, questionnaires are designed in Phase IV, and product posttesting begins in Phase VI. MOEs are determined during the planning process in Phase I, and are often refined during Phase II. However, the actual data collation and analyses with respect to the MOEs are completed during this final phase.

PSYCHOLOGICAL OPERATIONS ASSESSMENT TEAM

6-9. The initial stages of PSYOP planning for military operations are characterized by an informal flow of information between the combatant command's J-3 PSYOP staff officer, IO planners, and the regional POB. It is common, as planning intensifies, for the combatant commander to request a POAT to assist the J-3 PSYOP staff officer during critical stages of deliberate planning or any CAP.

6-10. A POAT is requested by the combatant commander's staff through USSOCOM under the following circumstances: A determination is made that a planning evolution has progressed to the point where the combatant command's J-3 PSYOP staff officer requires additional expertise to prepare a plan, where execution planning is beginning, or when a crisis action team (CAT) is established. A POAT is most effective when incorporated into planning as early as possible.

6-11. A POAT serves many purposes. POATs are deployed for minor crises through major conflicts to determine the feasibility of PSYOP application and the supporting requirements. A POAT augments a unified command or a JTF staff to provide a full range of PSYOP planning support (Figure 6-2, page 92). The size and composition of a POAT are mission-based and situation-dependent. A POAT may consist of as little as one operational planner to as many as twelve or more personnel including tactical, print, broadcast, communications, and logistical planners, as well as an SSD analyst.

A POAT focuses its assessment of the operational area on eight primary areas:

- TAs.
- Production facilities.
- Communications infrastructure.
- Competing media.
- Available indigenous commercial and government information holders.
- Logistics support.
- Dissemination capabilities.
- Tactical considerations.

Figure 6-2. POAT Eight Primary Areas of Assessment

6-12. A POAT assesses HN capabilities and availability of production media (print, radio, and TV), means of distribution, and broadcast equipment. The communications representative determines the availability and practicality of electronic distribution methods for PSYOP products within the AO, both intertheater and intratheater. During the assessment, the logistical representative identifies and coordinates for the necessary memorandums of agreement (MOAs) and contracts to ensure support from the HN, interagencies, and other Services. A POAT has the following capabilities:

- Assesses the friendly and enemy PSYOP situation, current propaganda, and PSYOP potential.
- Analyzes supported unit's mission and PSYOP requirements and relays these to the supporting PSYOP unit.
- Writes PSYOP supporting plans, the PSYOP estimate of the situation, and other documents, as required.
- Evaluates the mission, enemy, terrain and weather, troops and support available, time available, civil considerations (METT-TC) and the particular needs for tactical PSYOP.
- Evaluates printing needs, in-country supplies, and possible printing facilities and other assets.
- Evaluates audio and audiovisual requirements to determine broadcast needs, locations, frequency availability, ranges, and other requirements.
- Evaluates bandwidth capability and availability, and communications capabilities to implement reachback.

- Determines and coordinates all communication requirements for PSYOP forces.
- Conducts initial analysis.
- Conducts rapid deployment.
- Serves, when directed, as the advanced echelon (ADVON) for follow-on PSYOP forces.

6-13. A POAT has the following limitations:

- No product development capability.
- No dissemination capability.
- Limited research and analytical capability.
- No tactical loudspeaker capability.
- Restricted size and composition in many cases.

6-14. The POAT is a planning element, not an operational unit. The POAT may become a part of the operations portion of the unit when the unit deploys; however, the primary function of the POAT is to determine the need for, and to plan for, PSYOP activity—not conduct the activity. If the POAT becomes a PSE or POTF, then the limitations listed above must be mitigated. The mission of the POAT concludes when it either transforms into a PSE or POTF or completes all requirements.

> *During URGENT FURY, improvisation replaced planning for PSYOP and CA activities. The small amount of PSYOP planning was conducted by LANTCOM level and above. However, this planning was inadequate, which may have been attributed to the timing of PSYOP and CA involvement or, more likely, to the inadequacy of contingency plans… By the time PSYOP personnel became actively involved in the planning process, the "thinking stage" had passed, and everything was required "right now"… On arrival in Grenada, PSYOP elements had to spend a day trying to determine where to go and to whom to report.*
>
> TRADOC, "Operation URGENT FURY"

PSYOP SUPPORT ELEMENT

6-15. The PSE is a tailored element that can provide PSYOP support. PSEs do not contain organic command and control capability; therefore, command relationships must be clearly defined. The size, composition, and capability of the PSE are determined by the requirements of the supported commander. A PSE is not designed to provide full-spectrum PSYOP capability; reachback is critical for its mission success. A PSE is often established for smaller-scale missions where the requirements do not justify a POTF with its functional component command status. A PSE differs from a POTF in that it is not a separate functional command. A PSE normally works for the supported force S-3/G-3/J-3 or, in some cases, a government agency such as a Country Team. A PSE can work independent of or subordinate to a POTF and, as such, provides PSYOP planners with a flexible option to meet mission requirements. A PSE can provide a full range of PSYOP support options, ranging from a small C2 planning capability up to a more robust C2 structure normally provided by a POTF.

6-16. There are many considerations when developing the task organization of PSYOP forces. The complexity of the operation and the availability of forces will be the underlying considerations behind the establishment of a POTF as a stand-alone functional component command or the use of a PSE embedded within the supported unit G-3/S-3 or other element. The two main advantages of a POTF are its ability to provide full-spectrum PSYOP support and its designation as a component command with inherent C2, with resulting access to the commander. The POTF has a robust command and control element and includes all the staff sections. The PSE is a smaller tailored force that has the advantage of not needing all of the accompanying staff elements. It decreases significantly the numbers required from that of a POTF. The disadvantages of a PSE are that it cannot provide full-spectrum support, its reachback requirements are greater, and it can sometimes be buried in a supported unit's staff where it is difficult to obtain the direct access to the commander that is necessary for effective PSYOP. Table 6-1 gives a quick reference to the advantages and disadvantages of both the POTF and PSE models.

Table 6-1. Advantages and Disadvantages Between POTF and PSE

POTF	PSE
Advantages	Advantages
• Access to CDR.	• Minimal footprint.
• Greater support to task force.	• Less personnel impact.
• Priority of effort from home base.	• Reduced administrative/ logistics concerns.
• Less reliance on reach back.	• Focused purely on PSYOP.
• Inherent C2.	
Disadvantages	Disadvantages
• Increased logistical tail.	• Less access to CDR.
• Increased personnel.	• Lower priority of effort.
• Increased cost.	• Less capability to support.
• Large space requirement.	• More reliant on other assets.

6-17. A PSE often executes missions in support of a geographic combatant commander's TSCP or non-DOD agencies, usually under the auspices of peace operations (developed, coordinated, and overseen directly by the ASD[SO/LIC] as per DOD Directive 5111.10, *Assistant Secretary of Defense for Special Operations and Low-Intensity Conflict [ASD(SO/LIC)]*). As a result of an interagency decision meeting (23 November 1998) and Presidential Decision Directive (PDD) 68, *U.S. International Public Information (IPI)*, the term "PSYOP" was replaced with the less-sensitive term of "IMI." Subsequently, IMI is now the interagency term for PSYOP, although PSYOP is still used within DOD. Within the geographic combatant commander's AORs, other terms are sometimes used by the U.S. Country Teams to refer to those PSEs that directly support them. PSEs often support missions such as counterinsurgency, CD, and HMA.

6-18. The process for deploying a PSE is identical to that of deploying any forces in the absence of or prior to the establishment of a POTF. Once the PSE is deployed, C2 of a PSE passes to the theater combatant commander. The PSE operates under the day-to-day control of the DAO, senior military commander, or other representative designated by the U.S. Ambassador.

Product approval rests with the Ambassador or designated representative, typically the DCM or senior military commander.

6-19. The PSE provides PSYOP expertise to non-DOD agencies, such as the U.S. Country Teams, normally in support of peace operations. Its capabilities are similar to those of a POTF, with emphasis on interagency and regional expertise.

It's a bird. It's a plane. It's a new comic book starring Superman and Wonder Woman designed to teach children in Central America about land mines. The book, "El Asesino Escondido" ("The Hidden Killer"), was introduced June 11 at UNICEF House at UN headquarters in New York. Brian Sheridan, principal deputy to the assistant secretary of defense for special operations and low-intensity conflict, represented the Defense Department at the unveiling ceremony. He called the book a major step forward in the effort to protect children in Costa Rica, Nicaragua, and Honduras from the threat posed by land mines. Six hundred fifty thousand copies of the book—560,000 in Spanish and 90,000 in English—were published in the second partnership of DOD, UNICEF, and DC Comics, a division of the Time Warner Entertainment Co. A similar comic book was published in English and Eastern European languages to promote mine awareness in Bosnia-Herzegovina. First Lady Hillary Rodham Clinton introduced it in 1996 at the White House. Soldiers from the 1st PSYOP Battalion (Airborne), Fort Bragg, North Carolina, conducted assessments in Costa Rica, Nicaragua, and Honduras, provided background information and photos and recommended a story line to the creative staff at DC Comics. The collaboration ensured accuracy and that Central American children would be able to identify with the villages, countryside and clothing depicted in the new book. Once the story and artwork were completed, the battalion tested the comic book in Central America to see if it conveyed the intended message. Members of the Army's Special Forces, as well as the staffs of UNICEF, U.S. embassies and local governments, will work together to distribute the book throughout the region. Mine-awareness posters based on the comic book—170,000 in Spanish and 30,000 in

English—will be distributed in Latin America; similar posters were used in the Bosnia campaign.

DOD News Release, June 1998

TASK FORCE

6-20. If the POAT determines that the operation is large enough and requires a large amount of PSYOP support, then it will recommend the establishment of a POTF. The POTF brings together all PSYOP capabilities under robust C2, usually as a subordinate functional component command under a JTF. PSYOP units organize as a task force for two primary reasons—

- *First,* no single skill set—product development, product design, production, distribution, dissemination, tactical, or I/R—in the PSYOP force structure is capable, in isolation, of fulfilling complex mission requirements.
- *Second,* the variety of mission profiles prevents the development of a single, all-purpose organization; each mission requires a unique structure, task-organized to meet the supported commander's requirements.

6-21. Commanders conduct force tailoring to meet the requirements of each mission profile. In practice, units develop standing operating procedures (SOPs) with standardized force packages that are used as a basis for planning. This SOP provides a baseline from which to tailor the task force to respond rapidly in time-sensitive situations.

6-22. The force structure required to conduct the PSYOP process (planning, TAA, series development, product development and design, approval, production-distribution-dissemination, evaluation) varies depending on the size and complexity of the operation. For this reason, in peacetime, PSYOP units are task-organized along functional lines for administration, military occupational skill-specific training, and personnel and equipment resourcing. Just as the U.S. military fights as a joint team and the Army fights as a combined arms team, PSYOP commanders fight as a task force or subordinate functional component command. In the same manner that infantry and armor commanders seek to produce synergy—combat power greater than the sum of its parts—by operating in support of each other, so too does the PSYOP commander by combining regional, tactical, and dissemination assets into a task force. The full weight and effect of PSYOP forces are brought to bear only when the right mix of assets is used. This mix of capabilities is further strengthened by the addition of PSYOP-capable assets from the Air Force, the Navy, the Marines, OGAs, and friendly nations. This tailored force—the POTF—is the foundation for employing PSYOP forces in large-scale contingencies.

6-23. The flexibility inherent in the POTF mindset is essential to the employment of PSYOP forces that routinely attempt to influence a wide array of TAs in peace, conflict, and war. TAs often range from information-savvy audiences in technologically advanced nations to victims of natural disasters who want only basic information on food, medicine, and shelter. TAs that PSYOP must address in the current asymmetric environment of the 21st century are extremely varied and necessitate a flexible operational force structure.

6-24. To successfully operate in this unpredictable environment, the United States responds with as many elements of national power as possible. In addition to military power, the U.S. government will use diplomatic, informational, and economic resources to advance national objectives. Also, when possible, the United States will endeavor to include friends and allies. Therefore, planners should assume that the military component of a U.S. response must adapt to the joint, interagency, and multinational environments. The POTF concept (Figure 6-3, page 99) allows commanders to tailor their force to meet the specific requirements of complex missions as they emerge and evolve.

6-25. The POTF includes all U.S. Army PSYOP assets that are designated in war plans or OPORDs as a task force (by the combatant commander or CJTF) to support a particular operation. In some cases, a POTF may directly support a major component command upon release by the combatant commander. The POTF provides PSYOP to the overall joint or combined operation at the strategic, operational, and tactical levels. It

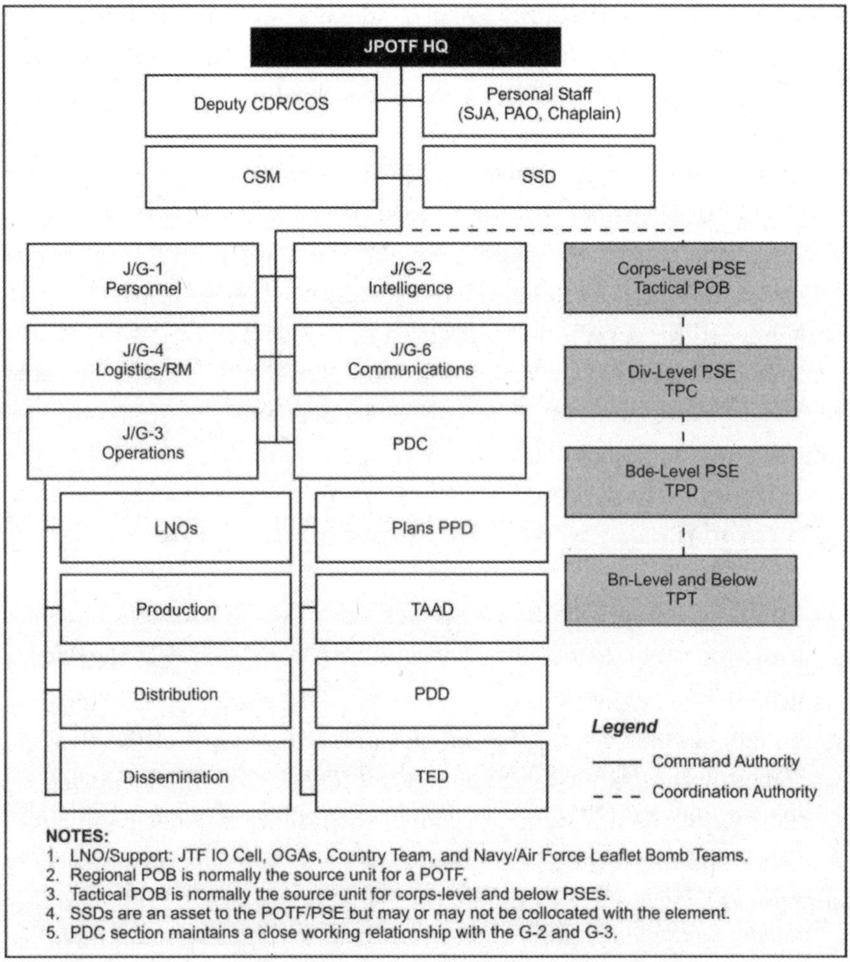

Figure 6-3. Example of POTF Organization

coordinates with each of the Service components, functional components, and staff elements to determine PSYOP requirements based on mission analysis. The POTF works closely with the U.S. Country Team, other USG officials, coalition officials, and international organizations. Finally, it coordinates strategic-level PSYOP with the combatant commander and the joint staff.

6-26. Mission requirements will dictate the organizational structure of the POTF and the functions it will perform. The POTF may include

PSYOP forces from the Active Army and RC as well as from the various Services. When directed by the appropriate authority, with assigned, attached, OPCON or TACON joint forces, the POTF may be chartered as a JPOTF per criteria established in JPs 3-0, 5-0, and 5-00.2. The POTF may also be organized as a CJPOTF if coalition partners provide PSYOP staff personnel and forces to support the operation IAW joint and combined directives (as per above mentioned JPs). A PSYOP group HQ may provide the commander and staff needed to support a large-scale operation. A regionally-oriented POB will normally provide the nucleus of the POTF, including the commander, staff, PDC, SSD, and required liaison elements. The PSYOP tactical and dissemination battalions provide additional assets, as required, to complete the POTF organization. As a tailored force, POTFs have ranged in size from 20 to 600 personnel.

> *Psychological operations were a key Battlefield Operating System used extensively to support Unified Task Force (UNITAF) Somalia operations. In order to maximize the PSYOP impact, we established a Joint PSYOP Task Force under the supervision of the Director of Operations, integrated PSYOP into all plans and operations, and limited the PSYOP focus to the operational and tactical levels. Psychological operations do not accomplish missions alone. They work best when they are combined with and integrated in an overall theater campaign plan. In Operation RESTORE HOPE, we were successful in doing that.*
>
> Major General Zinni, U.S. Marine Corps,
> Director of Operations, Unified Task Force Somalia

6-27. The POTF plans and conducts PSYOP in support of a combatant commander, CJTF, or corps. As a force-tailored package, a POTF brings the combined capabilities of all PSYOP forces. Regional, tactical, and dissemination assets, as well as assets from other Services, task-organize before deployment of each mission to make sure the range of capabilities is available to the supported commander. The overall capabilities of a POTF are listed in the following paragraphs, although the degree and mix of these forces will depend on the mission.

COMMAND AND CONTROL

6-28. In addition to U.S. Army PSYOP forces, the POTF exercises C2 of those PSYOP assets assigned, attached, and under OPCON and TACON from other Services and, when applicable, from other nations. Further, although tactical PSYOP units are usually attached to maneuver commanders, the POTF normally has coordinating authority with tactical forces for developing, designing, producing, and disseminating PSYOP products. This procedure allows PSYOP forces to meet the maneuver commander's requirements more effectively, while ensuring continuity with the objectives and intent of the President and/or SecDef, combatant commander, or CJTF.

6-29. The POTF is normally under OPCON of the geographic combatant commander or CJTF and is capable of commanding and controlling PSYOP forces and functions. Tactical POBs and companies are normally attached to maneuver elements (Armies, corps, Service components, divisions, brigades), but dissemination POBs elements normally operate as major subordinate units or detachments of the POTF. Multipurpose assets that are primarily PSYOP platforms, such as the 193d Special Operations Wing's (SOW's) EC-130E/J COMMANDO SOLO and other aerial platforms, usually remain under OPCON of their Service or functional component, but coordinating authority is given to the POTF for execution, planning, and coordination. Normally, the POTF also has coordinating authority over tactical units. Chapter III of JP 0-2 discusses command relationships and other authorities.

COMMUNICATIONS

6-30. Army signal doctrine dictates that communications responsibilities go from "higher to lower," from "left to right," and from supporting to supported unit. However, PSYOP communications requirements are inherently joint and interagency in nature, and as a theater asset, a POTF will require connectivity from the deployed location back to the sustaining base. This requirement may place extraordinary communications demands upon an undeveloped theater in time of crisis. Therefore, commanders should adhere to the following principles when planning PSYOP in a theater. There are three distinct functions that must be supported by communications in order for PSYOP forces to be successful:

- C2.
- Intelligence.
- Distribution.

6-31. When a POTF is employed, the force possesses its own organic equipment and communications personnel from the dissemination POB and may be augmented by the 112th Signal Battalion of the Special Operations Support Command (SOSCOM) if required. However, the POTF may require additional augmentation and assistance from the supported combatant commander, SOC, or JTF. Therefore, it is often preferable to collocate the POTF with the supported headquarters to facilitate coordinated use of the higher headquarters' capabilities.

6-32. For C2 and intelligence, PSYOP forces will normally operate or coordinate for periodic access of the following systems and networks:

- LAN of the supported command.
- SIPRNET and Nonsecure Internet Protocol Router Network (NIPRNET) of the Defense Information Systems Network (DISN).

6-33. Through the SIPRNET, PSYOP planners will use the Global Command and Control System (GCCS). PSYOP forces will require JDISS equipment, a transportable workstation, and a communications suite that electronically extends communications to the POTF forward. The GCCS will provide access to the following systems as a minimum:

- *The Joint Operation Planning and Execution System.* This system is used by PSYOP planners for planning, time-phased force deployment data (TPFDD), or strategic deployment planning.
- *The Global Reconnaissance Information System (GRIS).* GRIS supports the planning and scheduling of reconnaissance operations.
- *The Evacuation System.* This system displays information about U.S. citizens located outside the United States.

- *The Global Status of Resources and Training (GSORT).* This system provides detailed data regarding the status and training of all DOD units' equipment and training. The GSORT system is an excellent tool to determine forces in position and capable of executing PSYACTs in support of PSYOP units.
- *The Joint Maritime Command Information System (JMCIS).* This database offers a fused or common operational picture of the operational battlespace.
- *The Theater Analysis and Replanning Graphical Execution Toolkit.* This system provides required access to documents, information sources, analysis tools, multimedia, and teleconferencing tools to ensure continuity of planning for PSYOP forces.
- *The Joint Worldwide Intelligence Communications System (JWICS).* The JWICS will be used to obtain access to the sensitive compartmented information portion of DISN. This data includes photographs, maps, and images. PSYOP forces commonly use this system to query intelligence analysts and archives developed by the intelligence community, such as intelligence link (INTELINK), Special Operations Command Research, Analysis, and Threat Evaluation System (SOCRATES), POAS, Situational Influence Assessment Model (SIAM), and Community On-Line Intelligence System for End-Users and Mangers (COLISEUM).
- *The Contingency Theater Automated Planning System and Air Tasking Order.* These systems provide PSYOP forces visibility over planned air operations conducted at the direction of the POTF.

As the use of GCCS has grown, the PSYOP forces' use of GCCS has grown as well. Each new system fielded has applications for PSYOP forces.

6-34. PSYOP forces require access to the Automatic Digital Network (AUTODIN) to send and receive general service (GENSER) messages or communications and Defense Switched Network (DSN) for worldwide interbase telecommunications within the DOD.

6-35. PSYOP forces have the capability to integrate their tactical communications devices into future and legacy Army communications networks. PSYOP forces will always bring their own video distribution network to the JOA or AOR. Currently, only PSYOP forces possess the capability to distribute large video files on a global scale. However, PSYOP forces must coordinate the use of these systems with the supported combatant commander's J-6. Some networks used and planned for use by PSYOP forces include the following:

- Single Channel Tactical Satellite.
- International Maritime Satellite.
- The Global Broadcast System/Joint Intra-theater Injection System.
- The PSYOP Distribution System.
- C, X, and Ku Band Satellite Communications.

6-36. PSYOP forces may depend upon the communications capabilities of other Service component commands to support the PSYOP mission. For example, should U.S. Navy TARBS dissemination capabilities be used, the Naval Component Command must provide organic compatible communications to receive audio products for dissemination. However, should SOF aviation units, such as the 193d SOW, EC-130E/J COMMANDO SOLO, deploy to an undeveloped intermediate staging base, PSYOP forces will provide required distribution communications in order for the 193d SOW to receive and disseminate audio and video PSYOP products.

6-37. PSYOP forces always coordinate bandwidth requirements with the J-6 of the supported geographic combatant commander, not the supported JTF. This early coordination ensures support throughout the AOR and deconflicts PSYOP communications requirements at the earliest possible time during contingency planning. The supported combatant commander and/or JTF may elect to use PSYOP communications equipment and allocated bandwidth for purposes other than PSYOP distribution when this equipment and/or bandwidth is not being used.

6-38. PSYOP communicators must coordinate and manage the frequency spectrum under the direction of the J-6 of the supported combatant commander and JTF. PSYOP communicators participate in the Joint Restricted Frequency List (JRFL) coordination process with the supported command's J-6, like any other functional or Service component command. C2 frequencies are assigned via this process. However, the coordination between the electronic warfare officer, the primary electronic support planner of the IO cell, the J-2, the primary electronic surveillance planner of the combatant commander or JTF, and the PSYOP communicator, must be fully integrated to ensure capabilities are maximized and priorities are established. Allocation of targeted frequencies for dissemination must be coordinated as part of the electronic countermeasures support to the targeting process, in conjunction with the intelligence, operations, and fire support communities.

> *For the first time in U.S. history, American psywarriors employed electronic psywar in the field, in September 1944. Engineers of the 1st Radio Section of the 1st MRBC recorded POW interviews for front-line broadcasts, and reproduced the sound effects of vast numbers of tanks and other motor vehicles for Allied armored units in attempts to mislead German intelligence and lower enemy morale.*
>
> USASOC History Office

6-39. Current organic communications capabilities, when using reachback techniques, require high bandwidth for the distribution of PSYOP video, audio, and data. PSYOP forces may use ground or air couriers to physically deliver PSYOP products to tactical PSYOP units for dissemination when sufficient bandwidth or equipment is unavailable. This technique can cause the PSYOP products to be untimely and, consequently, ineffective.

6-40. PSYOP require continuous access to emerging technologies (for example, Global Broadcast Satellite; proliferation of fiber optic cable and high-bandwidth technologies, such as Asynchronous Transfer Mode and Synchronous Optical Network; and high-bandwidth military and commercial satellite systems). This access enables PSYOP forces to plan and implement a more robust reachback capability for the efficient distribution of PSYOP products.

6-41. The PDS provides PSYOP forces an organic, high-bandwidth-capable, secure/nonsecure, fully interoperable, multichannel satellite communications (SATCOM) system for product distribution to link all PSYOP elements on a near-real-time basis. The PDS enables battlespace commanders to receive timely, situation-specific PSYOP products. The PDS also enables video production units to craft required products and disseminators to quickly receive and relay commercial broadcast-quality products to the intended audience.

6-42. PSYOP forces organize in a variety of configurations in order to accomplish the wide and varied nature of the operations they support. PSYOP commanders ensure that the necessary mix of regional, tactical, and dissemination assets are employed to accomplish the mission.

COMMUNICATIONS SUPPORT ELEMENT

6-43. The communications support element (CSE) normally consists of organic PSYOP communications sections from the dissemination POBs, augmented as needed by USASOC signal units (for example, 112th Signal Battalion). When part of a JPOTF, this element may also include Joint Forces Command (JFCOM) JCSE.

6-44. The dissemination POBs comprise the majority of the production element. When part of a JPOTF, this element may include the Navy's Audiovisual Unit-286 (AVU-286), which has TV production capabilities, a team from the Joint Combat Camera Center (JCCC), and other contracted support, as needed.

6-45. The MOC at Fort Bragg, North Carolina, is also an asset of the dissemination POB and is normally in DS of the supported combatant commander or CJTF for the conduct of PSYOP during crises. The MOC usually remains in DS during a crisis until a theater media operations center (TMOC) is established in the AOR or JOA. The MOC then reverts to GS. The MOC is also in GS to all PSYOP forces for execution of peacetime operations. These activities are done in support of the GCCs' TSCP. TMOCs usually only support a POTF and are deployed as part of a POTF during a crisis in an AOR or JOA. Each TMOC normally consists of eight personnel and is usually located in large, populated cities with access to communications, airfields, media, and commercial information outlets. Ideally, TMOCs are as close as possible to the POTF.

6-46. The dissemination POBs provide the core of broadcast capabilities for the POTF; however, they are often augmented with contracted support, as required. Also, when part of a JPOTF, other dissemination assets may include the 193d SOW (EC-130E/J COMMANDO SOLO), the 16th SOW (COMBAT TALON), and FIWC's TARBS.

6-47. When part of a JPOTF, the IO support team may include representatives from JWAC, JIOC (with a Traveler system), and 1st IO Command Land (Chapter 7 further explains these organizations). This team collocates with the JTF J-2 or JTF IO cell in a sensitive compartmented information facility (SCIF) and provides dedicated support to the POTF.

6-48. The POTF staff sections (roles and responsibilities are outlined in FM 3-05.301) normally consist of core staff elements from the regional POB, with staff augmentation from the POG and other USASOC or Army assets such as intelligence, security, finance, communications, and signal support. Also, when part of a JPOTF, the staff sections may include augmentation from JFCOM JCSE (in the J-6), Air Intelligence Agency (AIA) (J-2), and the Naval Air Warfare Center Aircraft Division (NAWCAD) (contractual and PSYOP-specific maintenance support in the logistics and maintenance/J-4).

> *As early as August of 1964, almost one year before the activation of the Joint U.S. Public Affairs Office (JUSPAO), General William Westmoreland told a CA and PSYOP conference that "psychological warfare and civic action are the very essence of the counterinsurgency campaign here in Vietnam...you cannot win this war by military means alone." Westmoreland's successor, Creighton Abrams, is known to have sent down guidelines to the 4th Psychological Operations Group that resulted in the drawing up of no less than 17 leaflets along those lines. In fact, the interest in PSYOP went all the way up to the Presidency; weekly reports from JUSPAO were sent to the White House, as well as to the Pentagon and the Ambassador in Saigon. In sum, it is a myth that the United States, stubbornly fixated on a World War II-style conventional war, was unaware of the "other war."*
>
> USASOC History Office

To be maximally effective, PSYOP units should be provided with linguists from the outset. In both Somalia and Bosnia interventions, the PSYOP units that were deployed had no linguists for a period of several weeks and had to rely on prerecorded messages for their loudspeaker teams. Such prerecorded messages proved of limited utility. In Somalia, only three or four of the numerous prerecorded messages that were prepared prior to deployment could be used in the situation the PSYOP teams actually encountered. As one JULLS report put it: "There is no substitute for live broadcasts. Messages have to be exact, down to inflection and emphasis."

Arroyo Center (Rand Corporation) Report,
"Information-Related Operations in
Smaller-Scale Contingencies," 1998

REACHBACK

6-49. To make best use of all available technologies and resources, PSYOP use reachback capabilities. This concept allows a portion of PSYOP forces that support forward-deployed elements to transfer products and ideas instantaneously. They use secure communications links including the SIPRNET, the Psychological Operations automated system (POAS), the PDS and the Army Battlefield Control System (ABCS).

6-50. Under the reachback concept, a portion of a regional PSYOP battalion normally remains with the POTF (Rear) (or, if so chartered, the JTF [Rear]) and the MOC, depending on mission requirements. Here, personnel work on long-range planning and develop PSYOP products based on mission requirements and then provide them to the POTF (Forward). The remainder of the PDCs and dissemination POBs will continue to deploy to the AO to develop, produce, and disseminate PSYOP products at the tactical and operational levels, using PSYOP internal assets or other military or civilian assets in the AO. Portions of the POTF (Rear), however, may move forward as the situation dictates.

6-51. This reachback capability offers the POTF several advantages. The number of personnel deployed forward and the accompanying "footprint" are reduced, resulting in cost reduction and enhanced force protection.

Those PSYOP forces needed to coordinate with the commander and JTF or CJTF and to disseminate products (for example, using loudspeaker, print, radio, or TV means) deploy forward with the POTF. Thus, the mixing of reachback technology with the PSYOP force structure, organization, equipment, and C2 can help the POTF commander to better monitor the PSYOP plan through centralized planning with decentralized execution. This capability requires the combatant commander's communication sections to plan for and integrate the PDS into their existing command, control, communications, computers, and intelligence (C4I) structure and to provide dedicated bandwidth to the POTF.

6-52. Reachback allows a POTF commander to leverage existing fusion centers and information systems as well as product development resources such as video and audio libraries and PSYOP forces located in other countries. This ability to reach back into national intelligence databases and fusion centers allows for near-real-time access to raw and finished intelligence products and real-time exchange (for example, dedicated Joint Deployable Intelligence Support System [JDISS] connectivity collocated with the JIC of the supported JTF), which is critical not only during the PSYOP development process (TA analysis), but also during dissemination and evaluation.

Chapter 7

INFORMATION OPERATIONS

Information operations are the employment of the core capabilities of electronic warfare, computer network operations, Psychological Operations, military deception, and operations security, in concert with specified supporting and related capabilities, to affect or defend information and information systems, and to influence decision making (FM 3-13). The Army definition recognizes that individuals and groups in the information environment, especially the AO and area of interest, affect military operations. Threats and targets in the information environment include adversaries and non-adversaries alike. The decision-making processes of friendly, adversary, and other organizations are the focus of IO.

GENERAL

7-1. IO, by their nature, are joint. Each Service component contributes to an integrated whole synchronized by the joint force headquarters.

7-2. The IO cell at joint force HQ deconflicts and synchronizes joint force IO. All Service components are represented. The joint force IO cell synchronizes all the Service-specific IO elements and related activities to achieve unity of effort supporting the joint force. The IO cell, located in the main command post, brings together representatives of organizations responsible for all IO elements and related activities. Related activities include any organizations able to contribute to achieving IO objectives. PA and CMO are always related activities; commanders may designate others. The IO cell also includes representatives of special and coordinating staff sections as the mission requires. All battlefield operating systems are represented. The primary function of an IO cell is to synchronize IO throughout the operations process.

7-3. The core elements specified supporting and related capabilities of IO are similar to the battlefield operating systems. They are independent activities that, when taken together and synchronized, constitute IO (Figure 7-1).

CORE

- OPSEC.
- PSYOP.
- Military Deception.
- Electronic Warfare.
  - Electronic Attack.
  - Electronic Protection.
  - Electronic Warfare Support.
- Computer Network Operations.
  - Computer Network Attack.
  - Computer Network Defense.

SUPPORTING

- Physical Destruction.
- Information Assurance.
- Physical Security.
- Counterintelligence.
- Counterdeception.
- Counterpropaganda.

IO-RELATED ACTIVITIES

- PA.
- CMO.

Figure 7-1. Elements of IO

PSYOP AND INFORMATION OPERATIONS

7-4. PSYOP function not only as an integral capability of IO, but also benefit from IO activities, capitalizing on the growing sophistication, connectivity, and reliance on information technology. Understanding this relationship is critical to realizing the mutual benefits of integrating the skills and capabilities of PSYOP with the other facets of IO. This chapter addresses this integration and discusses the reciprocal roles of both areas.

ORGANIZATION AND FUNCTIONS

7-5. Usually, the combatant command, JTF, or Service and functional component commands will establish a cell or staff to facilitate the IO process. This cell coordinates and synchronizes IO capabilities and related activities into joint force operations. This cell will usually have representatives for every core and supporting element and related activity of IO, the supported general staff, the supporting combatant commands, and all subordinate Service and functional components. It will also include members from the Civil Affairs operations (CAO), CI, special technical operations, and SJA communities. PSYOP forces will normally have a representative in the IO cell at all these HQ. PSYOP representatives to the IO cell are already assigned to the Army HQ (Army service component commands (ASCC), corps, division, or group) as planners. Others may come directly from the supporting PSYOP units, when required. However, the PSYOP representative performs duties in the IO cell in addition to those normally required as a liaison from the POTF or PSE.

7-6. PSYOP officers may be assigned duties as chief of IO in the IO cell they support. However, when this occurs, another PSYOP officer should be assigned from the POTF or PSE for IO planning, as the assigned officer will rarely be able to perform functions simultaneously as a PSYOP officer and as chief of the IO cell. To participate in the IO cell, PSYOP officers should have a valid security clearance at the top secret-sensitive compartmented information (TS-SCI) level. In the IO cell, the PSYOP representative integrates, coordinates, deconflicts, and synchronizes the use of PSYOP. He also includes multinational information activities within a CJTF's AOR or JOA that may support IO. This representative serves as the entry point for liaison from the POTF or PSE and the in-theater multinational PSYOP cells and PSYOP detachments, as appropriate. It is important to note that this officer does not plan PSYOP. The PSYOP representative does not have the time or resources to adequately plan PSYOP in isolation. Rather, he facilitates and integrates PSYOP.

7-7. The PSYOP staff officer or NCO provides expertise within the appropriate staff element at the component command or unified command. At the Army corps and division level, the Deputy Chief of Staff (DCS), G-7 IO, is responsible for coordinating and synchronizing the elements of IO.

At the unified command level and other than Army Service component level, IO and its elements are coordinated in the IO cell within the J-3 or G-3. The PSYOP staff officer or NCO plans, coordinates, validates, and reports PSYOP force deployments theaterwide in response to the SecDef, the joint staff, and other operational and contingency requirements. The staff officer or NCO integrates directly with the J-3 or G-3/G-7 staff and ensures PSYOP inclusion and integration in IO.

7-8. The PSYOP representative in the IO cell performs the following functions:

- Integrates PSYOP plans with IO plans.
- Coordinates PSYOP support from the POTF or PSE.
- Serves as liaison for information flow from the POTF or PSE to the supported IO cell.
- Leverages IO cell assets as one of the sources for PSYOP information requirements.

7-9. PSYOP and IO are mutually supportive and beneficial. Each enhances the other's capability and mission effectiveness. Full integration and synergy of PSYOP and IO activities must occur to maximize their effect. This synergy of activities ensures consistency of message and optimizes credibility. Because of its complexity and inherent risks, PSYOP must be planned, conducted, and represented on staffs by PSYOP personnel. Additionally, because PSYOP are a means by which the commander speaks to approved TAs in the JOA, PSYOP planners/liaisons require periodic and direct access to the commander.

7-10. Just as IO can enhance and facilitate PSYOP, PSYOP can contribute to the achievement of a supported commander's IO objectives. PSYOP personnel assigned or attached to a supported command (working in the operations staff [J-3, G-7, S-3] of the supported command) coordinate, synchronize, and deconflict PSYOP with IO. They participate through continuous coordination and liaison as staff members in an IO cell and targeting meetings. PSYOP personnel advise the supported commander on all aspects of PSYOP and recommend PSYACTs and PSYOP-enabling actions. PSYOP supports IO by—

- Changing the behavior of foreign TAs.
- Providing feedback on the effectiveness of IO. PSYOP personnel can collect information in the performance of assigned duties that, although not specifically related to PSYOP, may indicate effectiveness in another aspect of a supported command's IO plan.
- Conducting PSYOP programs to accomplish the POs, which support the commander's IO objectives. For example, an IO objective may include denying certain frequencies to adversaries. PSYOP can develop radio products to broadcast on these frequencies and effectively deny their use to adversaries, amplifying the effect of IO efforts. For example, PSYOP programs can exploit the efforts of CMO, such as medical programs and engineering projects.

7-11. Although IO support agencies are not qualified or resourced to plan or execute PSYOP, they can facilitate PSYOP in a number of ways that enable the operations to be as timely and tailored to the situation as possible. They can assist in synchronizing PSYOP with other capabilities and related activities of IO to ensure unity of effort. IO agencies can access other resources, especially dissemination tools, to make PSYOP series execution significantly more effective.

7-12. PSYOP are an essential tool in both C2-attack and C2-protect operations. As one of the five core elements, PSYOP integrate their activities with those of electronic warfare (EW), military deception, OPSEC, and computer network operations to create a synergistic effect. PSYOP serve as a focal point for persuasion and influence strategy. PSYOP forces facilitate targeting by analyzing the various factors that affect and influence the behavior of an adversary, such as religion, ethnicity, economics, politics, culture, region, history, leadership, geography, demographics, and national interests. They use this analysis to nominate targets in order to change the behavior of TAs in order to deter conflict (whenever possible), facilitate military operations, and to support and communicate national objectives.

7-13. During C2-attack, PSYOP can drive a wedge between the adversary's leadership and its populace to undermine the adversary leadership's confidence and effectiveness. Through the proliferation of discrete messages, demonstrations, and surrender appeals to adversary C4I collectors, PSYOP forces magnify the image of U.S. superiority. In C2-protect, the main objective of PSYOP is to minimize the effects of propaganda and disinformation campaigns against U.S. forces. PSYOP units must work closely with other IO elements and PA and CMO strategists to maximize the advantage of IO.

INFORMATION OPERATIONS SUPPORT TO THE POTF OR PSE

7-14. Joint and Service-specific IO support elements and organizations offer the following capabilities and technologies that enhance and facilitate PSYOP in support of a commander. An IO cell supports the POTF or PSE of a combatant commander or CJTF that intends to employ PSYOP in a JOA or AOR. The cell could be expected to perform some of the following tasks:

- Provide access to databases and links to other Services and to OGAs that can provide alternate distribution or dissemination means and intelligence support to PSYOP forces.
- Provide access to organizations that conduct media, propagation, and spectrum analysis, as well as modeling.
- Provide systems and links to facilitate the collection of PSYOP impact indicators that relate to MOEs of supporting PSYOP programs.
- Provide access to organizations that provide critical personality profiling and human factor analysis.
- Obtain special information not usually available through DOD intelligence systems for PSYOP use upon request.
- Coordinate and synchronize PSYOP with other IO activities and CJTF or combatant command operations.
- Augment dissemination of PSYOP series via nonstandard dissemination assets or platforms.
- Facilitate PSYOP contingency planning by coordinating resources to support the PSYOP scheme of maneuver.
- Assist in coordination and synchronization of operational and tactical PSYOP with strategic information campaigns, programs, or activities.
- Ensure synergy with deception, EW, OPSEC, physical destruction capabilities of IO, and related activities of PAO and CA.

- Provide responsive access and use of classified and compartmented information and programs for PSYOP forces, as required.

INFORMATION OPERATIONS AGENCIES

7-15. Several agencies are set up and structured to support the IO process. Each of the Services has an IO unit to directly support their needs and several are chartered to support the joint community as well. Most IO coordinating agencies are a subset of their respective Service's intelligence organization, and they coordinate and facilitate IO. Most IO support agencies remain intelligence resourced and oriented. This trait is occasionally a problem, as information is often compartmented, and ties to field personnel are limited. Listed below are some of the organizations with which PSYOP units may require continuous coordination.

THE JOINT INFORMATION OPERATIONS CENTER

7-16. This center is under the command of the United States Strategic Command (USTRATCOM). JIOC has supported PSYOP directly during every major contingency since the Gulf War and is collocated with the AIA at Kelly Air Force Base (AFB), Texas. A minimum of four PSYOP officers are always assigned to the JIOC. JIOC's charter is to provide full-spectrum IO support to operational commanders. The JIOC supports the integration of the constituent elements of IO: OPSEC, PSYOP, military deception, EW, and destruction. It also supports the noncombat military applications of information warfare (IW) throughout the planning and execution phases of operations. The JIOC provides this DS using deployable teams in the following priority order of support:

- Unified commands.
- Joint task forces (subordinate unified commands).
- Service component commanders.
- Functional component commanders (for example, POTF).

7-17. PSYOP officers serve on many of the teams that support the regional combatant commanders. PSYOP officers can serve as "information brokers" for the POTF, PSE, or peacetime PSYOP planners by providing timely packaged information that the POTF, PSE, or planner depends upon to operate. When IO support is expected to be a major part of the PSYOP mission, PSYOP planners should consider requesting DS liaison from the JIOC. This officer need not be PSYOP-qualified. However, he should be knowledgeable in his duties as an information broker.

1ST IO COMMAND LAND

7-18. The Army established 1st IO Command (Land [L]), formerly Land Information Warfare Activity (LIWA) to integrate IO across the Army. The 1st IO Command (L) specifically provides tailored support to the land component commands. The 1st IO Command (L) is part of the U.S. Army Intelligence and Security Command. The 1st IO Command (L) receives operational taskings from the Director of Operations, Readiness and Mobilization, Headquarters Department of the Army. The 1st IO Command (L) provides tailored field support teams (FSTs) to help operational and tactical battle staffs integrate IO with plans, operations, and exercises. The FSTs provide a linkage back to the 1st IO Command (L) Information Dominance Center (IDC) at Fort Belvoir, Virginia. The IDC can provide access to DOD IO intelligence as well as IO-related intelligence from other government agencies. When deployed, the 1st IO Command (L) FSTs are integrated into the supported command's IO staff.

THE NAVAL INFORMATION WARFARE ACTIVITY

7-19. NIWA is located at Fort Meade, Maryland. It is the Navy's principal technical agent to research, assess, develop, and prototype information warfare capabilities. This recently created activity supports the development capabilities encompassing all aspects of information warfare (IW) attack, protect, and exploit. A key focus of efforts in this line is providing tactical commanders with an IW mission planning, analysis, and command and control targeting system (IMPACTS) tool. NIWA is the Navy's interface with other Service and national IW organizations, working closely with the FIWC to develop IW technical capabilities for Navy and joint operations. NIWA is the Navy counterpart to 1st IO Command (L). PSYOP forces will normally work closely with this activity when the JTF is under Navy or Marine Corps command, or when the Navy Service component requires direct PSYOP support.

7-20. The FIWC, located at Little Creek Amphibious Base, Virginia Beach, Virginia, is the Navy IW Center of Excellence. The FIWC became operational on 1 October 1995. As of July 2002, FIWC has been subordinate to the Naval Network Warfare Command. The FIWC is responsible to provide computer incident response, vulnerability analysis and assistance, and incident measurement protect services to fleet and shore establishments. The FIWC provides the facilities, equipment, and personnel for directing the defensive IW program, including detecting and responding to computer attacks.

THE AIR FORCE INFORMATION WARFARE CENTER

7-21. The AIA of the United States Air Force (USAF) commands this center. AFIWC is located at Kelly AFB, Texas. This agency is the Air Force counterpart to 1st IO Command (L), and has a PSYOP cell within its organization. This PSYOP cell routinely augments the POTF or PSE with intelligence assets. PSYOP forces work with AFIWC most closely when the JTF is under Air Force command, or when the Air Force Service component requires direct PSYOP support.

JOINT WARFARE ANALYSIS CENTER

7-22. This center assists the combatant commanders in preparation and analysis of joint operation plans and analysis of weapon effectiveness. It provides analysis of engineering and scientific data and integrates operational analysis with intelligence. JWAC can also use the SIAM, in coordination with PSYOP organizations, as a means to determine pressure points in a coordinated perception management campaign. The JWAC will normally support a JTF through the supported combatant command. PSYOP uses JWAC routinely to analyze and evaluate the telecommunications network in a JOA or AOR. This organization has proved most capable of synthesizing information and building workable models that facilitate PSYOP's telecommunications requirements.

JOINT PROGRAM OFFICE FOR SPECIAL TECHNICAL COUNTERMEASURES

7-23. This organization has the ability to assess infrastructure dependencies and the potential to impact on military operations resulting from disruptions to key infrastructure components. Specific infrastructures include electric power, natural gas, liquid petroleum, transportation, and telecommunications. Joint Program Office for Special Technical Countermeasures (JPOSTC) also conducts technical assessments of emerging special technologies to determine their potential impacts to military and civilian systems and proposes countermeasure solutions or response options, as warranted. PSYOP must work with JPOSTC to ensure continuity of effort when addressing impacts of telecommunications. PSYOP may be completely dependent on commercial infrastructures within a JOA. JPOSTC can make recommendations that not only deconflict but also facilitate the use of civilian infrastructure telecommunications by PSYOP. JPOSTC may also help PSYOP forces with countermeasures against adversary jamming of PSYOP transmissions while helping identify optimal frequencies for transmission.

JOINT SPECTRUM CENTER

7-24. This center provides DS to the JFC through the joint force IO cell in several areas. JSC personnel conduct locational and technical characteristics analyses about friendly force communications and assist in JRFL deconfliction. The JSC resolves operational interference and jamming incidents and provides data regarding foreign C4I frequency and location data. Historically, the JSC information has been critical to PSYOP mission success. The JSC propagation analysis for PSYOP dissemination platforms, technical analysis of the electromagnetic spectrum, and infrastructure networks are critical base products that PSYOP forces require to build a dissemination network in the JOA or AOR. JRFL deconfliction is also essential to the success of a POTF.

JOINT COMMUNICATIONS SECURITY MONITOR ACTIVITY

7-25. Joint Communications Security Monitor Activity (JCMA) provides information security monitoring and analysis of friendly C4I systems to ensure security. PSYOP products should be considered extremely sensitive, if not classified, before dissemination. The POTF or PSE will often be the outlet for many operational and strategic policies set by the President and/or SecDef and coalitions. If this information is released prematurely, it can have an overarching effect that could be detrimental to operations of the combatant commander and, indeed, the USG. Therefore, it is essential that PSYOP planners coordinate JCMA support.

JOINT COMMUNICATIONS SUPPORT ELEMENT

7-26. The JCSE augments unit communications using a wide array of tactical and commercial communications equipment. Routinely, PSYOP faces a communications dilemma when determining a secure location for PSYOP product development, production, and dissemination. Methods of distribution to dissemination platforms within a JOA or AOR present a special challenge, since JOAs and AORs are never the same in this respect. Thus, PSYOP may require special augmentation to distribute products to disseminators. JCSE can help in this regard. However, JCSE resources are extremely limited. PSYOP planners should request its support early during the planning stages of an operation or mission.

HUMAN FACTORS ANALYSIS CENTER

7-27. This center is a joint Defense Intelligence Agency (DIA) and Central Intelligence Agency (CIA) organization that analyzes social behaviors and human factors of groups and individuals. HFAC personnel study the impact indicators of information. They also act as the intelligence fusion center for human factors analysis. The 4th POG(A) SSDs provide PSYOP-specific information and analysis to this organization routinely. The HFAC is an important organization to PSYOP. Detailed information regarding social and human behavior is available from this organization to PSYOP personnel anywhere in the world.

Chapter 8

INTELLIGENCE SUPPORT

Conducting and evaluating effective PSYOP requires extensive intelligence support. Essentially, PSYOP intelligence is processed information about selected foreign TAs. Intelligence support for PSYOP focuses on the conditions and behavior of these groups, and answers IRs from PSYOP forces. It is based on knowledge of an entire AO, scope of mission, society, geography, demographics, and weather. Furthermore, intelligence identifies threat PSYOP activities and can provide the basis for recommending countermeasures. This chapter identifies those intelligence systems, products, and information that PSYOP personnel need to support the commander. FM 3-05.301; FM 3-13; FM 3-05.102, *Army Special Operations Forces Intelligence;* and FM 34-1, *Intelligence and Electronic Warfare Operations,* provide the details regarding intelligence support to PSYOP.

INTELLIGENCE REQUIREMENTS

8-1. Commanders must ensure that their personnel are an integral part of the supported command's intelligence center. As a minimum, PSYOP liaison personnel should work in or closely with the supported unit's intelligence organization. Its intelligence personnel should be tasked to extract PSYOP-related information from all incoming reports, paying particular attention to IRs.

8-2. The *senior intelligence officer (SIO)* for a PSYOP unit works closely with the commander to develop intelligence requirements. The SIO then collects information from Army, joint, interagency, and coalition sources—formal and informal. PSYOP analysts are also important contributors to the intelligence process. They provide both information and finished intelligence studies, while the SIO leverages organic and nonorganic assets to answer the command information needs.

8-3. PSYOP forces develop IRs while planning and conducting IPB, and executing the PSYOP process to include evaluating MOE.

ENVIRONMENTAL ANALYSIS

8-4. In this category, the analyst takes a long-term view of each of the 14 political-military factors and addresses their role over time in influencing a society. This information may be very detailed; however, it is relatively enduring and is usually compiled over an extended period of time. The SSD is the primary source of analysis of the PSYOP environment.

TARGET AUDIENCE ANALYSIS

8-5. This category of intelligence involves looking at the 14 political-military factors as the initial conceptual framework for conducting thorough TAA. TAA is completed during Phase II of the PSYOP process and requires significant amounts of information. Many IRs are identified during this process and must be integrated into the supported command's collection efforts. When complete this intelligence allows PSYOP forces to identify, analyze, and select specific foreign audiences and communicators. This information must be frequently updated; it is the information that allows a PSYOP unit to target a particular TA with various media in order to achieve an objective. In addition to the SSDs, intelligence needed to conduct TAA comes from many sources, including tactical PSYOP Soldiers in face-to-face contact with TAs.

USE OF DIGITAL SYSTEMS BY PSYOP FORCES

8-6. Digital systems are a commander's principal tool in collecting, transporting, processing, disseminating, and protecting data. Digital systems are the information exchange and decision support subsystems within the C2 support system of the total force. The continuous need for information to support PSYOP is the basis for the development of PSYOP-specific digital systems. PSYOP also require access to the ABCS for a continuous flow of information. Availability of information can make the difference between success and failure of a PSYOP mission. The data must get to the right place, on time, in a format that is quickly usable by the intended recipients, in order to generate appropriate actions. Special military operations conducted in peace, stability operations, support operations, and war differ significantly from conventional operations. PSYOP operators must be able to communicate long-range, anywhere in the world and at any time, while remaining completely interoperable with joint and Army systems. Appendix D includes detail on digital systems.

DEVELOPING PSYOP-SPECIFIC INTELLIGENCE REQUIREMENTS

8-7. From the moment operations are contemplated, PSYOP planners launch a continuing, interactive process to develop and refine the commander's estimate of the situation. Essentially, PSYOP IRs focus on particular TAs. This information includes the identity, location, conditions, vulnerabilities, accessibilities, and impact indicators of a designated.

8-8. Determining specifically how any given TA is going to react to joint force operations is difficult and a great challenge confronting PSYOP specialists and PSYOP commanders. The factor that makes determination of future behavior so difficult is the process of action and reaction that will occur between a military force and its TAs. Friendly actions or even preparation will, if detected, cause a reaction by the TA. These efforts have been referred to as the "process of interaction." Estimating the outcome of the process of interaction requires the PSYOP officer to know what future friendly actions are planned, forecast many different factors involved in the actions, and to determine the most likely effects of these interactions.

8-9. The formal development of PSYOP IRs begins in Step 2 of the Army's MDMP (mission analysis) with the identification of the initial CCIR. The CCIR directly affect the success or failure of the mission and they are time-sensitive in that they drive decisions at decision points. The key question is, "What does the commander need to know in a specific situation to make a particular decision in a timely manner?"

8-10. Development of PSYOP IRs continues in Step 4 of the MDMP (COA analysis) during the war-gaming process. The war-gaming process is a repetitive process of action, reaction, and counteraction during which the S-2 role-plays the TA (or enemy commander, as appropriate). By trying to win the war game for the enemy, he ensures that the staff fully addresses friendly responses for each enemy's COA. The result of this process is a refined and finalized CCIR list ready for submission with the plan under development. Once developed and submitted, the SIO (J-2/S-2) continually checks on their status and works with the commander and S-3 to develop CCIR that reflect a dynamic operational environment.

PSYOP AND THE IPB PROCESS

8-11. The Army IPB process involves the execution of four steps; although PSYOP have special considerations, PSYOP personnel follow the same steps as the rest of the Army. PSYOP require extensive intelligence collection to conduct vigorous PSYOP-relevant analyses that delve into potential TAs and the PSYOP environment. The following paragraphs focus on the PSYOP potion of the Army IPB steps:

- *Step 1. Define the battlefield environment.* For PSYOP, the emphasis during this first step is to identify weather, terrain, infrastructure, and potential TAs within the AOR. These functions are most often completed by G-2 or S-2 in conjunction with the PSYOP planner, POAT, and PPD. Identification of these essential elements is done during initial IPB.
- *Step 2. Describe the battlefield's effects.* For PSYOP, Step 2 of IPB is where analysis is conducted. The G-2 or S-2 must analyze the weather and terrain and determine how these will affect the dissemination of PSYOP products by both friendly and hostile forces. Infrastructure analysis for PSYOP considers the information environment and the media outlets that disseminate information. This analysis must determine which outlets are available for use by friendly PSYOP forces and those that are being used by opponent forces. The POTF or PSE S-2 or G-2, in conjunction with the supported unit's intelligence section, is primarily responsible for this portion of Step 2. The analysis of the

potential TAs that were identified in Step 1 is done by the TAAD. The TAAD takes the PTAs from Step 1 of IPB and the SPO that was written during planning and begins to analyze each target set and SPO combination to determine the vulnerabilities, lines of persuasion, susceptibilities, accessibilities, and effectiveness of each TA. This is the target audience analysis process (TAAP). This process determines each TA's ability to affect the battlefield. The TAAD will determine the ability of each TA to influence the PSYOP and supported commander's stated objectives.

- *Step 3. Evaluate the threat.* PSYOP specialists concern themselves with propaganda analysis and counterpropaganda during this stage of IPB. They monitor the competing agencies within the AOR who are disseminating information and determine what effect that information will have on the conduct of the operation. This analysis is largely done by the TAAD but with significant assistance from the G-2 or S-2 who will be interfacing with the various intelligence agencies to obtain PSYOP-relevant information. A technique, which facilitates propaganda analysis, is to have TAAD and G-2 or S-2 personnel located near one another. This function of propaganda analysis is peculiar to PSYOP IPB and, when done effectively, can be of great interest and assistance to a supported commander.
- *Step 4. Determine threat COAs.* The information gained from the first three steps in the IPB process allows the PSYOP planner to determine what the threat's propaganda objectives are, what propaganda COAs are available to the threat, which COA is most likely to occur within the given environment, and a feasible method of countering that propaganda.

8-12. Although the PSYOP IPB builds on the IPB of the higher HQ, it is oriented on the human aspects of the situation and the capabilities of audiences to receive and be influenced by information. The process looks at TAs within and outside the AOR that can affect the supported commander's objectives. PSYOP IPB is research-intensive and requires that attention be given to areas of the battlespace that are not historically considered. PSYOP IPB must consider not only opposing forces but also neutral and friendly audiences that may also impact the mission.

PROPAGANDA ANALYSIS AND COUNTERPROPAGANDA

8-13. The process by which U.S. military personnel determine when, if, and how to address propaganda can be divided into two basic tasks with subordinate tasks. Propaganda analysis encompasses collecting, processing and analyzing; counterpropaganda encompasses advising and executing.

PLANNING

8-14. Counterpropaganda planning is not a separate step, but is embedded throughout the PSYOP process. In the initial PSYOP tab/annex, planners and analysts begin to identify PSYOP objectives, SPOs, and potential TAs that will reduce the effectiveness of an opponent's propaganda campaign.

8-15. As the operation commences and plans are realized, planners and analysts attempt to identify indicators of any potential propaganda campaign developing. As indicators arrive, they are integrated into the intelligence and TAA process. Analysts attempt to confirm or deny their initial anticipated opponent plan and fill in any holes.

8-16. PSYOP series are planned and developed. Planners, analysts, and product developers begin to embed potential counterpropaganda lines of persuasion into TAAWs and ultimately into series. This proactive measure will assist in setting the stage for any later counterpropaganda operations.

COLLECTING

8-17. PSYOP personnel must use all available assets to collect the wide variety of information and propaganda existing in an area. Due to the sheer volume of information and potential sources, PSYOP forces do not have the organic ability to collect all available information. In addition, PSYOP personnel may be lured by the obvious propaganda appearing in the AO and miss collecting the more subtle and potentially effective propaganda being disseminated through the local media. Adversaries aware of PSYOP capabilities in the supported force may deliberately disseminate obvious propaganda to draw PSYOP personnel away from other events or information.

8-18. Media analysis is the structured, deliberate tracking and analysis of opponent and neutral media (TV, radio, Internet, and print).

Properly performed media analysis, although time-consuming and linguist-intensive, can identify trends and become predictive when the supported force considers a potentially unpopular activity. To be truly effective, media analysis must be conducted on a daily basis. PSYOP units usually do not have the organic personnel sufficient to accomplish this task. The TAAD of the PDC is best suited for conducting media analysis. Some organizations capable of conducting media analysis or sources are—

- *Intelligence organizations.* The J/G/S-2 sections have access to hostile media reporting and can assist in the analysis.
- *PA.* PA personnel and units frequently review and analyze media reports at the international and local levels. These analyses are often produced for the supported commander on a regular basis.
- *DOS.* Most U.S. Embassies have information officers (formerly known as United States Information Service [USIS] personnel) who collect and analyze international and local media reports.
- *Foreign Broadcast Information Service (FBIS).* FBIS reports are detailed and methodical in their analysis; however, there is usually a 24-hour delay in the receipt of the detailed reports. FBIS is an excellent resource, but may not cover all media in the AO; often they will report only on the larger media outlets.
- *International organizations and nongovernmental organizations (NGOs).* Many of these organizations conduct media-monitoring activities. In certain peacekeeping missions, some of these organizations are chartered with the task of media monitoring. Frequently, these organizations have significant expertise in the area and can provide valuable information and analysis.
- *Local media.* PSYOP personnel often work with the local media on a regular basis. In the course of routine business, PSYOP personnel can acquire valuable information concerning media reporting in the AO.
- *Internet.* Many media outlets maintain Web sites on the Internet. These sites frequently have the most recent editions of their reports posted in both the local language and in other languages.

8-19. The collection task presents several significant challenges: time, personnel, and integration. Time is a challenge because the analysis of propaganda and information often requires translation and careful studying. The use of outside sources can assist in overcoming this challenge. Personnel shortages and multiple requirements within the PSYOP forces present challenges for leaders in terms of prioritization of tasks. Again, the effective use of outside personnel and organizations will assist PSYOP forces in overcoming the shortage of personnel. PSYOP personnel must identify and coordinate with all available collection assets and integrate their capabilities.

PROCESSING

8-20. Processing opponent information and propaganda refers to the movement of the information through non-PSYOP and PSYOP channels. PSYOP personnel must ensure that their supported unit HQ and all of its subordinate units understand where suspected opponent propaganda and information is sent. All collection agencies must know that PSYOP units have the mission of analyzing opponent propaganda and information. Once in the PSYOP force, the G-2 or intelligence representative logs the item and keeps a copy, if necessary. The propaganda or information should pass to the PDC in the POTF or the TPDD in a TPC. Although the plans and programs section or detachment initially receives the suspected propaganda, ultimately the TAAD or target audience analysis team (TAAT) receives the product and begins the detailed analysis of it.

ANALYZING

8-21. When analyzing propaganda, PSYOP personnel work with two levels of analysis: the analysis of individual items of propaganda and propaganda program analysis.

8-22. Individual item analysis is conducted by PSYOP Soldiers using the source, content, audience, media, effects (SCAME) approach. The SCAME process is discussed in detail in FM 3-05.301.

PROGRAM ANALYSIS

8-23. Analysis of an opponent's propaganda program begins with what the PSYOP unit anticipates will happen. The collection of information confirms or denies the presence of such a program and enables the PSYOP analyst to identify the opponent's plan. This analysis involves searches in the international and local media, detailed propaganda analysis as items arrive, and TA actions and reactions. The lines of persuasion, TA and objectives all build to complete a "picture" for the PSYOP analyst.

8-24. Once PSYOP personnel suspect that a propaganda program is present in the AO, they must begin to analyze and anticipate the program. Individual product analysis feeds the program analysis and can clarify missing information. Program analysis is critical to the PSYOP unit because this analysis will serve as the basis for deciding when, if, and how to execute counterpropaganda operations.

8-25. PSYOP analysts then try to fit these pieces together to form a picture of the opponent's plan. Once the opponent's plan is verified, PSYOP personnel can begin to counter it by anticipating actions and reactions and disseminating series in advance of expected opponent propaganda.

ADVISING

8-26. PSYOP personnel advise the supported commander and coordinating staff of the current situation regarding the use or anticipated use of propaganda in the AO. PSYOP personnel advise commanders on the recommended defense against propaganda and recommend the appropriate material to be included in command information programs. This task also includes advice on available options for use of counterpropaganda based on—

- Propaganda analysis.
- Current intelligence.
- Planning considerations (discussed in the following section on counterpropaganda).
- Impact of propaganda.

COUNTERING

8-27. Part of the challenge of counterpropaganda is deciding whether or not to execute a counterpropaganda program in an active sense. Due to constraints, silence may be an option. It may be far more damaging to initiate a weak counterpropaganda plan and have it fail than to employ the silent option.

ORGANIC CAPABILITIES

8-28. PSYOP forces possess limited capabilities to collect, process, integrate, analyze, evaluate, and interpret PSYOP-relevant information for use by supported geographic combatant command, JTFs, component commands, other OGAs, and other intelligence organizations.

RESEARCH AND ANALYSIS DIVISION

8-29. The DCO/RACA manages the Research and Analysis (R&A) Division of the Active Army POG that supports all PSYOP groups and their subordinate elements. The DCO/RACA represents the commander in the intelligence production cycle, directs special projects and analyses to support contingencies and special actions, and supervises Department of Army civilian intelligence analysts assigned to the SSD.

STRATEGIC STUDIES DETACHMENT

8-30. A SSD, organic to the R&A Division, supports each regional PSYOP battalion. The SSDs provide comprehensive analysis of the PSYOP environment. SSD analysts, possessing advanced academic degrees and language skills. They are responsible for the PSYOP portion of the Department of Defense Intelligence Production Program (DODIPP) by producing high-quality SPSs and SPAs and by writing the PSYOP appendix to the military capabilities study. The analysts conduct thorough research and analysis of target countries, regions, groups, and issues to develop effective PSYOP. The detachments provide timely political, cultural, social, political-military, economic, and policy analyses to PSYOP commanders and their staffs, as well as to other agencies.

8-31. SSD analysts also assist in deliberate and contingency planning and deploy to support operations. The PSYOP studies and other SSD-generated analytical products are accessible through the POAS, which also provides the PSYOP community with access to various classified and unclassified databases. Commanders can access POAS through INTELINK and the sensitive compartmented information (SCI) INTELINK systems.

BATTALION S-2

8-32. Upon receipt of an impending PSYOP mission, the S-2 accesses existing databases and available intelligence products to support the mission. All available sources including the theater SOC J-2, the theater JIC, as well as national, coalition, HN, and supported units' resources. The S-2 also refers to the pertinent PSYOP studies produced by the SSD. These resources are processed and integrated as part of the PSYOP planning cycle. The PSYOP S-2—

- Accesses available intelligence to answer the commander's PIR and intelligence requirements.
- Ensures access to the intelligence assets and products required to support the commander.
- Ensures that the specialized products produced by PSYOP personnel are included in intelligence databases.
- Tasks organic and attached intelligence assets and forwards IRs to higher HQ.
- Integrates PSYOP intelligence efforts with other units and agencies.
- Maintains the current situation and environmental elements of the common operating picture.
- Identifies, confirms, and coordinates priorities for unit geographic area requirements for geospatial information and services (GI&S) products and services to support OPLANs and CONPLANs.

TA ANALYSIS DETACHMENT

8-33. The TAAD, an element of the regional PSYOP battalion, identifies TAs and analyzes their conditions, vulnerabilities, susceptibilities, accessibilities, and effectiveness. TAAD and SSD personnel combine their efforts to monitor and analyze intelligence and prepare in-depth TA analyses in the form of a TAAW. The TAAD also analyzes propaganda, misinformation, and opposing information against the United States or its forces to recommend countermeasures.

TESTING AND EVALUATION DETACHMENT

8-34. Elements of the TED conduct surveys, interviews, and panels to collect PSYOP-relevant information. These activities are different from tactical intelligence collection. They use techniques developed for market analysis, survey research, and human intelligence (HUMINT). The detachment's goal is to obtain specific information regarding a TA's demography, socioeconomic status, and conditions.

8-35. PSYOP series are subjected to analysis or scrutiny by opposing forces. It is important to have access to intelligence on the opposing forces propaganda. This information may be obtained through a combination of order of battle (OB) data, multidiscipline counterintelligence (MDCI) analysis, and information and analyses in PSYOP databases. PSYOP can also provide intelligence for use by the MDCI analysis and deception planning elements. This intelligence pertains to sociological prejudices or predilections of a targeted force that could be manipulated or exploited by a deception effort.

TACTICAL PSYOP BATTALION

8-36. The tactical POB provides direct PSYOP support to corps-level units and below. Tactical POBs develop, produce, and disseminate series assigned by the PSE or POTF. TPTs disseminate PSYOP products (for example, loudspeaker scripts, leaflets, handbills, and posters) in local areas and conduct face-to-face communications with the TAs. Tactical PSYOP units are able to collect information on the ground as they have direct access to the local populace and threat forces when disseminating products. TPTs provide the tactical POB and PSE or POTF with critical information on TA conditions.

8-37. A tactical PSYOP battalion also supports I/R operations. During conflict, detainees are continuous sources of current information of value for both PSYOP and intelligence operations. This battalion conducts tasks that support the overall PSYOP mission, to include—

- Screening the detainee facility population.
- Interviewing and surveying the camp population.
- Collecting PSYOP information.
- Disseminating reports of this information.
- Recording detainee surrender appeals.

PSYOP SUPPORT TO INTELLIGENCE

8-38. PSYOP units also produce specialized intelligence products to support a variety of other combat and intelligence missions and operations. PSYOP units develop these intelligence products by monitoring and assessing situations and evaluating their impact on specified target groups and national objectives. Finally, this information is combined with additional research on specific target groups.

8-39. The main focus of this production effort is on socioeconomic, political, and diplomatic factors. It also focuses on the military aspects of a region, situation, or group. These products include, but are not limited to—

- Strategic-level documents such as SPSs and SPAs.
- Operational- or tactical-level analyses on specific target groups.
- PSYOP reports and estimates.

8-40. Although PSYOP units primarily use these products to conduct their operations, the products also contain information and intelligence that is useful to other agencies. These products contain diverse information on social customs, enemy morale, and key nodes.

8-41. Through their specialized training and close contact with friendly and threat persons, PSYOP units can provide information of value to the PSYOP and intelligence efforts. PSYOP S-2s and other intelligence personnel must ensure this information is placed in intelligence channels. PSYOP units can conduct PSYOP assessments of I/R operations, coordinate the I/R intelligence collection activities, or otherwise support the information flow from threat areas.

NONORGANIC INTELLIGENCE SUPPORT

8-42. Organic intelligence support rarely provides all of the necessary information required for PSYOP units to plan, produce, disseminate, and evaluate the PSYOP effort. Therefore, PSYOP S-2s must leverage the available intelligence assets that are external to the PSYOP community. PSYOP depend on HUMINT, signal intelligence (SIGINT), imagery intelligence (IMINT), open-source intelligence (OSINT), technical intelligence (TECHINT), and counterintelligence (CI) support to plan their missions. These intelligence disciplines are discussed in the following paragraphs.

HUMAN INTELLIGENCE SUPPORT

8-43. Intelligence and information gathered from detainees, refugees, captured documents, and published materials often provide PSYOP elements with significant insights into the psychological situation in a specific area or within a target group. With consent and proper authority, these sources may be used to develop and test PSYOP products. In addition to organic HUMINT collectors, HUMINT support for PSYOP units is available from the supported theater's intelligence assets. Otherwise, HUMINT collectors are collocated at detainee collection points and holding facilities at division level and echelons above. Interrogation information is then incorporated into the all-source product. When PSYOP units need information for mission planning that only HUMINT collectors might provide, the PSYOP units must coordinate their requirements with the command that has HUMINT collectors.

SIGNALS INTELLIGENCE SUPPORT

8-44. SIGINT assets support PSYOP by providing SIGINT and EW products extracted from locating, monitoring, and transcribing threat communications. EW assets support PSYOP by locating and jamming threat PSYOP transmitters. These assets provide information and intelligence that help reveal enemy activities or plans so that PSYOP can develop effective countermeasures.

IMAGERY INTELLIGENCE SUPPORT

8-45. PSYOP units request IMINT support from the supported command. PSYOP analysts use IMINT to locate and determine the capabilities and operational status of transmitters or printing plants. PSYOP analysts also use IMINT to locate mobile target groups. By analyzing imagery of the location and architecture of key structures, analysts can determine the ethnic or religious makeup of a town or village. Other uses for IMINT products include identifying and evaluating operational capabilities of transportation networks, factories, and other public structures or systems. PSYOP analysts use IMINT to confirm or deny acts of rioting, acts of sabotage, demonstrations, and work slowdowns that are either the original PSYOP objective or an impact indicator of a PSYOP program or specific product.

OPEN-SOURCE INTELLIGENCE SUPPORT

8-46. OSINT—through publications, academics, and mass media—can provide information on natural disasters, biographic information, culture, historical context, weather, and even BDA. Open-source data can also be purchased for geospatial and mapping data. Less obvious is the use of open-source materials such as graffiti and taggings to identify gang turf or to gauge public opinion.

TECHNICAL INTELLIGENCE SUPPORT

8-47. PSYOP units can use TECHINT to focus their efforts on critical, highly technical threat units and installations. They can also identify alternative methods of PSYOP product dissemination through the analysis of the target population's information infrastructure. The Captured Materiel Exploitation Center (CMEC) or a battlefield TECHINT team at corps produces TECHINT products. TECHINT is incorporated into all-source intelligence products. Specific requests for TECHINT support are coordinated through the SOC J-2 to corps HQ or above.

COUNTERINTELLIGENCE SUPPORT

8-48. CI detects, evaluates, counteracts, or prevents foreign intelligence collection, subversion, sabotage, and terrorism. It determines security vulnerabilities and recommends countermeasures. CI operations support OPSEC, deception, PSYOP and force protection (FP).

OTHER NONORGANIC SUPPORT

8-49. PSYOP planners must have access to the latest GI&S and weather information to plan and conduct their assigned missions. This support is readily available from the outside sources described below. Additionally, PSYOP planners must integrate their requirements with supported units to benefit from the collection of other intelligence, such as measurement and signature intelligence (MASINT).

WEATHER

8-50. Weather and other environmental factors affect almost all PSYOP missions. Severe weather may degrade PSYOP dissemination efforts, as in the case of airborne leaflet drops. Sunspot activity can disrupt radio and TV broadcasts into a TA. Severe weather may also enhance PSYOP programs if it affects threat morale. Therefore, PSYOP units need accurate weather and environmental information. Required weather support includes—

- Forecasts of general weather conditions and specific elements of meteorological data, as described in the 24-hour forecast.
- Solar, geophysical information, and climatic studies and analysis.
- Weather advisories, warnings, and specialized weather products, as required.

8-51. The primary source for required weather intelligence support, to include specialized products, is the USAF 10th Combat Weather Squadron. This squadron is a component of the AFSOC that provides special operations weather detachments (SOWDs) for attachment to ARSOF units.

GI&S AND OTHER INTELLIGENCE PRODUCTS

8-52. PSYOP units, using their Department of Defense activity address code (DODAAC), may requisition standard National Imagery and Mapping Agency (NIMA) products through the Army supply system directly from Defense Logistics Agency (DLA). Intelligence products and services may also be requested from DIA. USASOC helps units obtain special GI&S products and services.

INTELLIGENCE SUPPORT FROM HIGHER ECHELONS

8-53. PSYOP missions often require intelligence support from higher echelons. National- and theater-level support is discussed in the following paragraphs.

NATIONAL SUPPORT

8-54. The majority of PSYOP missions, particularly at the strategic and operational levels, require access to intelligence information and materials produced at the national level. At the national level, non-DOD agencies such as the CIA and the DOS collect and produce valuable PSYOP-related intelligence. These agencies monitor all regions and are sanctioned to provide intelligence support to PSYOP. Within the DOD, the National Military Joint Intelligence Center (NMJIC), the National Ground Intelligence Center (NGIC), and the National Security Agency (NSA) provide worthwhile intelligence reports and products. These agencies have extensive knowledge of potential TA, and have databases and well-established collection frameworks that can support PSYOP efforts.

THEATER SUPPORT

8-55. The primary concern of the SOC J-2 is in-theater intelligence policy formulation, planning, and coordination for all deployed ARSOF, including PSYOP. The SOC J2—

- Ensures that sufficient intelligence support is available for each mission tasked by the SOC.
- Relies on the theater Service intelligence organizations to collect, produce, and disseminate intelligence to meet PSYOP requirements.
- Tasks subordinate SOF units and coordinates with higher and adjacent units to collect and report information in support of PSYOP intelligence requirements.

8-56. Theater OPORDs, OPLANs, campaign plans, and supporting PSYOP and intelligence annexes contain specific PSYOP intelligence requirements. Most of these requirements are validated and incorporated into PSYOP collection plans. (FM 34-1 and FM 34-2, *Collection Management and Synchronization Planning,* contain additional information on this subject.)

8-57. To meet some of these requirements, SIOs may need to reinforce or refocus available intelligence assets. Often, the PSYOP SIO must enter the intelligence system to access information or intelligence from other units, intelligence agencies, or sources at higher, lower, and adjacent echelons.

Chapter 9

SUPPORT AND SUSTAINMENT

It is the logisticians' enduring challenge to synchronize combat service support (CSS) activities with operational employment concepts. Never has this statement been truer than for the PSYOP logistician tasked to plan a concept of logistics support for PSYOP forces operating in a joint, international, or multinational environment. PSYOP forces operate from multiple bases ranging from CONUS through the communications zone (COMMZ) to the JOA. This task is made more complex by the increase in operations being conducted in geographic locations outside a theater support system.

This chapter outlines the primary tasks for logistics support to PSYOP forces, the concept for logistics support, responsibilities for support, and planning considerations.

CONCEPT

9-1. PSYOP units derive logistics support for operational elements from the ASCC. The ASCC, as prescribed by Title 10, USC 164, and Title 10, USC 167, states that the parent service retains responsibility for support of ARSOF. The ASCC develops the theater support plan that includes sustainment of PSYOP by theater logistics organizations.

9-2. The ASCC is responsible for reception, staging, onward movement, and integration (RSOI) and follow-on support and sustainment of in-theater Army forces, including PSYOP. The ASCC also provides support to Army forces in ISBs. PSYOP have some key differences that affect the type of support required for RSOI and sustainment. The following conditions occur often enough that they must receive special consideration during logistics planning:

- It is not unusual for forward-deployed PSYOP units to be isolated and in austere locations. Supply distribution is a key consideration.
- PSYOP units have significant amounts of unique equipment that require support through SO logistics channels.
- PSYOP units have extensive and unique contractual requirements.
- PSYOP units have extensive and unique requirements for financial support.

9-3. Support for PSYOP-specific items is coordinated through the SOTSE—a staff planning, coordinating, and facilitating element. This element is assigned to SOSCOM and attached by USASOC to the ASCC for duty within the ASCC G-3/G-4 staff to coordinate logistics support for all deployed ARSOF.

UNITED STATES ARMY SPECIAL OPERATIONS COMMAND

9-4. USASOC monitors ongoing logistics support to PSYOP forces and provides the initial support that may not be available from the ASCC. The organizations that perform these functions are—

- *Special Operations Support Command.* The SOSCOM plans, coordinates, and when required, executes CSS for PSYOP forces through its forward-deployed SOTSE and organic special operations support battalion (SOSB). The SOSCOM may also attach logistics LNOs to the POTF when its sustainment operations are expected to require complex joint, interagency and multinational, and contractual support.
- *Special Operations Theater Support Element.* The SOTSE has a coordination cell with the ASCC staff. It provides special operations staff expertise and coordinates access to the support infrastructure. It ensures PSYOP requirements are included in the support plan. It also provides the capability for deploying PSYOP to gain access to the theater Army support structures on arrival in-theater.

- *Special Operations Support Battalion.* When required, the 528th SOSB provides limited DS to PSYOP. It provides support from the early arrival and employment of PSYOP forces until the theater support structure capability can take over. The SOSB provides supply and maintenance support similar to that provided to conventional units. It also provides low-density and PSYOP-specific item support. The unit is capable of deploying anywhere in the world to provide early support. It provides support only until the theater support structure is established and capable of meeting PSYOP requirements. Once that occurs, the SOSB prepares to redeploy for another contingency.

THEATER SPECIAL OPERATIONS COMPONENT

9-5. The theater SOC supports PSYOP forces for any PSYOP-specific requirements the ASCC identifies as a shortfall. The theater SOC validates the SOR of PSYOP forces, and works closely with the unified command staff, the theater ASCC, and PSYOP logisticians to convey the PSYOP requirements.

9-6. The TSOC and PSYOP logisticians coordinate with the ASCC to develop plans and subsequent orders to implement directives the ASCC will issue to support the PSYOP forces assigned to the unified command. The TSOC, in conjunction with the POTF S-4, advises the ASCC commander on the appropriate command and support relationships for each PSYOP mission. The SOTSE keeps the SOSCOM and USASOC informed of the status of ASCC supporting plans.

9-7. The group or regional POB S-4 has the staff lead for logistics planning and execution. When not task-organized for an operational mission, the POG S-4 is the senior logistics officer, and the USACAPOC G-4 is the higher logistics authority. When task-organized for an operational mission, the POG S-4 will coordinate with the HQ having control to establish the logistics relationship; for example, a POTF that is COCOM to a theater combatant commander and in receipt of a JCS execute order in a CONUS garrison location, or one that is deployed OCONUS. The S-4 must arrange for continuity of logistics support during the transition between USASOC and theater control.

PLANNING

9-8. Planning can take two forms—deliberate planning and CAP. The following paragraphs provide more detail on these two forms of planning.

DELIBERATE PLANNING

9-9. PSYOP units and the ASCC can fully identify support requirements in OPLANs and CONPLANs from a bare base SOR, down to the user level based on an established set of planning assumptions. In this way, the ASCC coordinates the fulfillment of requirements from the support structure in the theater Army.

CRISIS ACTION PLANNING

9-10. In CAP, the requirements anticipated at the combatant command level dictate the amount of responsiveness and improvisation required to provide reactive, no-notice support and sustainment. Actual circumstances may dictate that preplanned requirements are modified or may generate new requirements that were unanticipated during the deliberate planning process.

STATEMENT OF REQUIREMENT

9-11. The SOR is the key to securing responsive support. SOR development begins with receipt of a WARNO from the supported TSOC through USSOCOM, USASOC, and USACAPOC, and/or during the deliberate planning process. Like the joint integrated prioritized target list (JIPTL) in the operational planning process, the SOR is recognized by Army and sister Service logisticians. The SOR is a powerful tool that PSYOP logisticians must master and use.

9-12. The intent of the SOR process is to identify logistics needs early in the planning cycle (Figure 9-1, page 145). The unit or task force coordinates through its higher HQ operations and logistics staff to provide the USASOC Deputy Chief of Staff for Operations and Plans (DCSOPS) (through USACAPOC) an initial list of requirements. USASOC DCSOPS tasks the Deputy Chief of Staff for Logistics (DCSLOG) to source all requirements.

9-13. A critical source of information the ASCC and the SOTSE need in their coordination and facilitation functions is the PSYOP SOR. The TSOC J-4 uses the ASCC OPLAN in preparing his CONPLAN for inclusion in the mission order. This approach allows the SOTSE time to review required support before the PSYOP mission unit submits the SOR. This review is especially critical in CAP and short-notice mission changes.

9-14. The SOR is a living document that requires periodic reevaluation and updating as requirements change. When a PSYOP unit receives a mission, it updates the standing SOR developed during the deliberate-planning process. The PSYOP commander uses this SOR to cross-level supplies needed at the assigned mission unit level. The SOR identifies, consolidates, and prioritizes in priority all unit requirements that exceed organic capabilities. The mission unit forwards it to the next-higher organization.

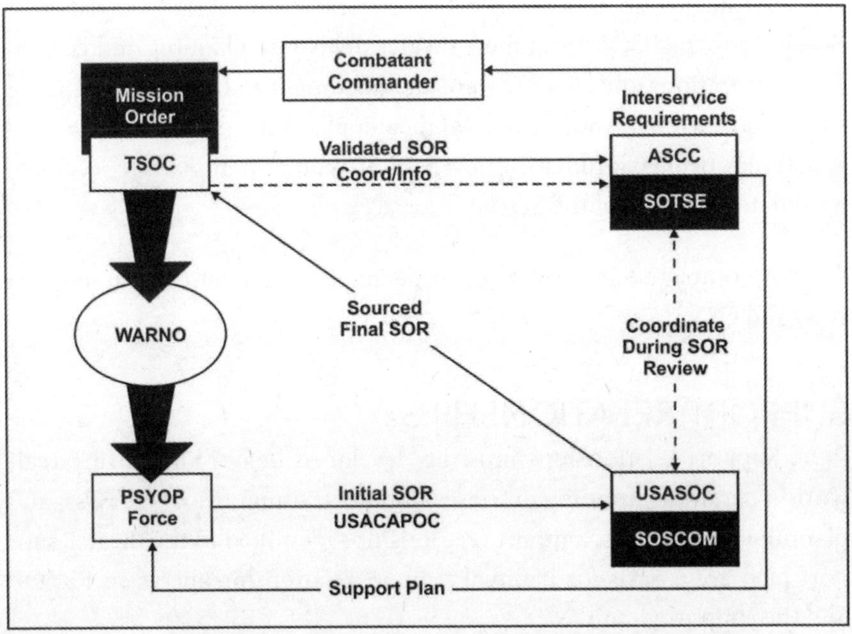

Figure 9-1. Statement of Requirement Process

9-15. At the next-higher level (group), the SOR starts the process into the operational channels (S-3/G-3). The operations and logistics sections review the SOR and direct or assist cross-leveling and transfer of needed items in the most expeditious way possible. This staff level then forwards the SOR to the next-higher level for any supplies and services still remaining on the SOR.

9-16. Any supplies and services that are not yet resourced on the SOR are again passed up the chain (USACAPOC). This level forwards a SOR requesting only the supplies and services not previously obtained.

9-17. At the next level (USASOC), the requirements that can be obtained within USASOC are coordinated and transferred. USASOC coordinates with Department of the Army HQ, Army Materiel Command (subordinate commands), other agencies, and major commands to source all requirements.

9-18. The development and coordination of a unit SOR is a dynamic process that occurs at multiple echelons concurrently. PSYOP logisticians develop a formal SOR to support theater deliberate planning and contingency operations and then forward the document to the theater SOC for validation. Given the fluid nature of theater planning, the theater SOC and ASCC may begin coordinating new ARSOF requirements before receipt of a validated revision of the SOR.

9-19. A complete SOR addresses in detail all aspects of combat support (CS) and CSS.

SUPPORT RELATIONSHIPS

9-20. Support relationships must be developed before and during real-world operations, training exercises, mobile training teams (MTTs), and planning conferences. Support relationships identified in the theater support plan are a basis for habitual support relationships between PSYOP and the supported unit.

THEATER LOGISTICS

9-21. The following information explains how logistics (supply, field services, maintenance, and transportation) is provided to PSYOP forces in a developed theater.

Supply

9-22. **Nonstandard/PSYOP-unique items.** PSYOP forces make unit requisitions and receive nonstandard PSYOP–unique equipment and items through the SOSB or the supply and transportation section for the supported unit in the case of supporting conventional forces. The SOSB fills the request from the theater or (in the case of certain non-DOD items) obtains the items through the SOC J-4.

9-23. **Classes I, II, III, IV, VI, and VII.** The supported unit's supply and transportation section requisitions, receives, and stores standard supplies from the supporting DS supply and service company in the tactical support center (TSC), area support group (ASG), or SOSB. All these classes of supplies (except bulk Class III) are demand items. The PSYOP unit submits a request through the supported unit's service detachment to the direct support unit (DSU).

9-24. **Bulk Class III.** These are scheduled item. The group or regional S-4 forecasts unit requirements through logistics channels to the TSC or ASG based on input from the battalions, companies, or PSEs. The TSC DCSLOG and theater Army material management command (TAMMC) develop a distribution plan to allocate fuel to subordinate units based on fuel availability (IAW theater OPLANs) and unit priorities.

9-25. **Class V.** The supported unit's supply and transportation section requests, draws, and stores conventional Class V supplies from the supporting ammunition supply point (ASP). A conventional ordnance ammunition company of the TSC ammunition group operates the ASP and uses supply point distribution. Class V supply is scheduled, not demanded. Based on input from PSYOP forces (PSE, POTF, and TPTs), the group S-3 must determine the group's operational requirements, primarily the unit basic load (UBL) and required supply rate. The S-3 then submits the requirements through operational channels for approval and allocation by the TSC DCSOPS. The TSC DCSLOG and TAMMC allocate scarce Class V items by computing a controlled supply rate based on guidance from the ASCC DCSOPS. Once the group commander receives his Class V allocation, he allocates it among his subordinate elements. Considering these allocations, the group and battalion S-3s approve unit Class V requests before the S-4s can fill them.

9-26. **Class VIII.** The group requisitions and receives its normal Class VIII supplies from the supporting DS medical treatment facility of the TSC U.S. Army Medical Command (MEDCOM). The medical facility uses a combination of unit and supply point distribution. Class VIII resupply is on demand. PSYOP forces, usually the TPTs, submit a request through their chain of command to the supported unit's medical supply sergeant, who forwards the request through medical channels to the medical facility. The facility either fills the request from its existing stocks or forwards the request to its supporting medical logistics (MEDLOG) unit. For bulk issue of Class VIII supplies to fill PSYOP operational requirements, the MEDCOM normally authorizes direct requisitioning from the MEDLOG unit.

9-27. **Class IX.** The supported unit's mechanical maintenance section requisitions, receives, and stores Class IX supplies from the their supporting DS maintenance company in the ASG. The DSU uses supply point distribution. Class IX resupply is on demand. The using unit, through its channels, submits its request to the mechanical maintenance section. The mechanical maintenance section forwards the request to the DSU. The DSU fills the request from its existing stocks or forwards the request to the TAMMC.

9-28. **Class X.** The supported unit's supply and transportation section receives and stores Class X supplies from the supporting TSC. The TSC uses a combination of unit, supply point, and throughput distribution. The using unit submits its request through the base S-5. The base S-5 forwards the request through logistics channels.

9-29. **Water.** The supported unit's supply and transportation section obtains potable and nonpotable water from local sources using organic equipment. When water requirements exceed the local supply, the section requisitions and draws water from a water supply point set up by the supporting DS supply and service company. The DSU uses supply point distribution.

9-30. **Maps.** The supported unit's supply and transportation section also requisitions and receives unclassified maps from the supporting DS supply and service company. The DSU obtains its unclassified maps from the appropriate TA map depot. Using units submit their requests to the S-2, who then consolidates them and forwards the requests through supply channels. The S-2 requisitions and receives classified maps and other classified intelligence products through intelligence channels.

FIELD SERVICES

9-31. Field services include mortuary affairs, airdrop, clothing exchange and bath, laundry, bread baking, textile and clothing renovation, and salvage. Mortuary affairs and airdrop are primary field services because they are essential to the sustainment of combat operations. All others are secondary field services.

9-32. PSYOP forces that sustain fatal casualties identify the human remains whenever possible, and place them in human-remains pouches. They then evacuate the remains through their supported unit's service detachment for further evacuation to the supporting mortuary affairs collection point. If the remains are NBC-contaminated, they and the pouches should be so marked. When a PSE cannot evacuate its dead, it conducts an emergency burial and reports the ten-digit grid of the burial to the supported unit and the group or battalion. The group or battalion S-4 submits a record of interment through mortuary affairs channels. Whenever possible, a unit chaplain, or the PSYOP commander conducts an appropriate service to honor the dead.

MAINTENANCE

9-33. PSYOP forces normally deploy with a limited organizational maintenance capability. They obtain DS and GS maintenance from the ASCC for Army common equipment. PSYOP forces obtain DS and GS maintenance for PSYOP-unique equipment from the USSOCOM Store Front System through the supporting SOTSE. The Store Front System is a unique and focused means to evacuate, repair, and replace SOF-unique equipment.

9-34. Tactical PSYOP forces are attached to the forces they support and therefore, receive all maintenance support from the force they are supporting. NAWCAD, an additional supplier, provides DS and GS maintenance for some PSYOP-unique equipment (upon request) directly to the user. It may also attach forces to a POTF for this purpose.

TRANSPORTATION

9-35. The unit S-4 coordinates for transportation support through the regional transportation movement office (TMO) of the theater Army movement control agency (TAMCA). The SOSB also may resolve transportation requirements. Tactical PSYOP forces submit requests through their supporting unit.

PERSONNEL SERVICE SUPPORT

9-36. PSS consists of five related areas—personnel management, public affairs, legal services, finance services, and religious support. PSYOP units plan and conduct most PSS activities using standard Army systems and procedures. PSYOP forces deal directly with the supported unit's personnel service company (PSC). Communications with the POTF or parent unit is key if support and services are not available.

CRITICAL PERSONNEL ACTIVITIES

9-37. Three critical military personnel activities directly support PSYOP operations. They are strength management, casualty management, and replacement operations.

Strength Management

9-38. Strength management determines personnel replacement requirements and influences personnel cross-leveling and replacement-distribution decisions. POG and POB S-1s use the deliberate Army personnel accounting and strength reporting system to maintain the unit's personnel database. They forward their daily personnel summaries and personnel requirement reports to the supporting PSC. The battalion S-1s provide copies of their reports to the group S-1 so he can prepare a consolidated report for the group commander and forward information copies to the SOC J-1 and ASCC. The supporting PSCs use these reports to submit requisitions for individual replacements to the TA Personnel Command (PERSCOM).

Casualty Management

9-39. The Army's casualty management system furnishes information to HQ, Department of the Army, for notifying next of kin and for supporting casualty and survivor assistance programs. By name, casualty reporting has far-reaching effects on the morale and the image of the Army. Casualty reporting must be 100 percent accurate, even at the expense of speedy reporting. Still, reporting should be as rapid as possible. The losing unit submits casualty feeder reports and, if required, witness statements to the supported unit's S-1 and courtesy copies to the POTF. The S-1 forwards them to the supporting PSC. The PSC manages open cases (for example, Soldiers missing in action) until final disposition is made. It prepares letters of sympathy for the commander's signature. It verifies the information before sending a formal individual casualty report. The battalion S-1 provides copies of all by-name casualty reports to the group S-1.

Replacement Operations

9-40. PSYOP replacement operations are the receipt, processing, and allocation of individual and small-unit (PSE or TPTs) replacements. Group obtains its replacements from PERSCOM using normal replacement procedures. The SOC commander coordinates with USSOCOM, USASOC, and the ASCC to set priorities of personnel fill. The S-1 and CSM distributes replacements based on the commander's priorities.

9-41. The ASCC can play a key role in requesting small-unit replacements. The ASCC arranges an intratheater transfer of PSYOP forces or coordinates to obtain PSYOP forces from CONUS.

OTHER PSS ACTIVITIES

9-42. *Postal operations* move, deliver, and collect personal and official mail. A DS postal platoon normally collocates with the PSC supporting the supported unit. The group and battalion S-1s set up internal procedures to collect and deliver mail. These procedures must include provisions for redirecting the mail of deceased, missing, and evacuated personnel. The S-1s must also make provisions for deployed personnel who cannot, due to operational reasons, receive or send mail.

9-43. *Finance operations* provide normal finance support and operational funds PSYOP forces (mainly the tactical forces attached to SOF) may need to execute their missions. A finance support unit normally collocates with the supporting PSC. The group and battalion S-1s can appoint Class A agents and set up internal procedures to meet the personal financial needs of their Soldiers. The group budget officer sets up procedures for the units to obtain and account for operational funds. In most cases, if the group or battalion do not appoint Class A agents but the supported unit has operational funding (OPFUND) requirements, the supported unit will appoint the Class A agent. Regardless of appointment authority, each individual who is appointed as a Class A agent must fully understand which payments are authorized and how to account for each transaction.

COMBAT HEALTH SUPPORT

9-44. When attached to SOF, PSYOP forces may have access to dispensaries, set up by the SF group and battalion surgeon, which provide preventive medicine services such as pest control, water quality surveillance, immunization, and drug prophylaxis activities. They can also conduct the general surveillance of military environments to identify actual or potential health hazards. SF preventive medicine specialists train and provide technical supervision of unit field sanitation teams. They can also participate in military civic action programs.

9-45. The Special Forces operational base (SFOB) and forward operational base (FOB) dispensaries provide veterinary services, such as food quality assurance inspections, dining facility sanitary inspections, and health services to military animals. SF veterinary specialists assist in the unit preventive medicine program. They can also participate in military civic action programs.

HOST-NATION SUPPORT

9-46. The PSYOP logistician must be familiar with conventional Army, ARSOF, and joint logistics. He must also be knowledgeable in securing support from multinational or HN sources. Host-nation support (HNS) is an additional means of meeting nonresourced CSS requirements during PSYOP operations. It should not, however, be the preferred means. HNS refers to support provided by a friendly country for U.S. military operations conducted within its borders based on mutually concluded agreements. It includes planning, negotiating for, and acquiring such support. HNS can include almost every aspect of CSS. HN personnel and organizations can perform many CSS functions as well as or better than their U.S. counterparts. The group or POTF commander, with the ASCC, must determine the functional types and levels of HNS he can accept without unduly jeopardizing OPSEC and mission accomplishment. The SOTSE can furnish the group S-4 with POCs of specific HN agencies or organizations that provide support in the theater. A similar source of CSS is foreign nation support (FNS). FNS includes the identification, coordination, and acquisition of foreign nation resources, such as supplies, materiel, and labor to support U.S. forces and operations. The difference between HNS and FNS is that FNS CSS is from a third country, not from the United States or the country in which the U.S. operations are taking place. All aspects for acquiring foreign nation CSS are the same as those provided for HNS.

UNDEVELOPED THEATER COMBAT SERVICE SUPPORT

9-47. An undeveloped theater does not have a significant U.S. theater sustainment base. FNS agreements are minimal or nonexistent. When a PSYOP unit deploys into an undeveloped theater, it must bring sufficient resources to survive and operate until the supported unit J/G/S-4 makes arrangements for HN and third-country support.

COMBAT SERVICE SUPPORT OPTIONS

9-48. Deployed PSYOP units in an undeveloped theater request CSS from the supported unit or may contact the POTF for PSYOP-specific resupply. They may also request a tailored support package from the SOSB to accompany them into the theater. The SOSB can then request directly from the CONUS wholesale logistics system (through the SOSB) and provide limited support and sustainment. They may also rely on the ASCC's contracting expertise to obtain support and sustainment. In practice, the solution may be some combination of all four options.

RECONSTITUTION

9-49. Regardless of the method used to reconstitute PSYOP forces, the request for additional personnel and equipment is sent ultimately to the POTF for action. Reconstitution operations are the actions taken to restore units to a combat-effective level. They involve more than a surge in normal sustainment operations. Unit and individual training, unit organization, and human factors heavily influence the reconstitution decision. The PSYOP commander two levels above the nonmission capable (NMC) unit makes the reconstitution decision. For example, the TPC commander advises the supported commander on how, or if, to reconstitute an NMC TPT. Commanders have two reconstitution options:

- *Reorganization* refers to the measures taken within an NMC unit to restore its own combat effectiveness, such as restoring C2, cross-leveling resources, and combining two or more NMC subordinate units to form a composite mission-capable PSE. The senior surviving member of the unit assumes command and quickly begins reorganization.
- *Regeneration* rebuilds an attrited unit through the wholesale replacement of personnel and materiel and mission-essential training. Replacement personnel and materiel may come from redistributed resources, reserves, or the resources of higher or supporting echelons. A commander can execute the options separately, but he most often executes them in combination. When a commander determines he cannot obtain the resources to restore an NMC unit to combat effectiveness, he may resort to redistribution as an alternative to reconstitution.

NOTE: Redistribution reduces an NMC unit to zero strength and transfers its remaining resources to other units. Redistribution is the least desirable option.

Appendix A

CATEGORIES OF PRODUCTS BY SOURCE

White, gray, and black products do not refer to anything inherent in the content of the product itself, but indicate the source of the product. Generally the content of a product is usually less truthful or completely fabricated when the source is misrepresented because the intent is to confuse or deceive the TA. Gray and black products are always covert because secrecy is key to their success. Credibility is key to successful products because the use and discovery of untruthful information irrevocably damages or destroys their and their originator's credibility.

OVERT PRODUCTS

A-1. A product that openly identifies its source is known as an overt product. Overt products are disseminated and acknowledged by the originator or by an accredited agency thereof. They are disseminated without intention to deceive the target audience as to where they originated.

WHITE PRODUCTS

A-2. White products are overt products. DOD forces use overt products in support of their operations.

Advantages

A-3. The advantages of white products are as follows:

- Add credibility because they are considered to be truthful.
- Convey messages that can easily be corroborated.

- Carry no risk of opponent discovering hidden meaning. Very difficult for opponent to compromise.
- Establish trust by openly giving the source of the information.
- Are easily coordinated, supported, and approved.
- Are based on factual information, thereby making opponent refutation difficult.
- Carry acknowledgement of the source; for example, USG adds credibility to the product based on perception of power, whether that power is diplomatic, informational, military, or economic.

Disadvantages

A-4. The disadvantages of white products are as follows:

- The opponent knows who the source is and can therefore easily direct their refutation.
- There are constraints on the types of information that can be included.
- Mitigating criticism of mistakes is more difficult.

COVERT PRODUCTS

A-5. Covert products require exceptional coordination, integration, and oversight. The operations are planned and conducted in such a manner that the responsible agency or government is not evident, and if uncovered, the sponsor can plausibly disclaim any involvement. Gray and black products are employed in covert operations.

GRAY PRODUCTS

A-6. Products that conceal and/or do not identify a source are known as gray products. Gray products are best used to support operational plans.

Advantages

A-7. The advantages of gray products are as follows:

- Overcome any existing negative orientation of the TA toward the originator.

- Use unusual themes without reflecting on the prestige of the originator.
- Introduce new themes based on vulnerabilities without identifying the true source. They can, therefore, be used for "trial" purposes.

Disadvantages

A-8. The disadvantages of gray products are as follows:

- They are limited by the difficulty of keeping their origins unknown yet authoritative.
- They may be vulnerable to critical analysis, thereby losing effectiveness and making them highly susceptible to opponent counterpropaganda.

BLACK PRODUCTS

A-9. Products that purport to emanate from a source other than the true one are known as black products. Black products are best used to support strategic plans.

Advantages

A-10. Advantages of black products are as follows:

- Purport to originate or originate within or near the opponent homeland, or opponent-held territory, and may provide immediate messages to a TA.
- The presumption of emanating from within an opponent country lends credibility and helps to demoralize the opponent by suggesting that there are dissident and disloyal elements within their ranks.
- Through the skillful use of terminology, format, and media, appear to be a part of the opponent's own propaganda effort, making the opponent appear to contradict himself, and forcing him to mount an expensive, difficult, and exploitable campaign that highlights the original black message.
- Their covert nature and the difficulty of identifying the true source hinder the opponent's ability to mitigate their effects.

Disadvantages

A-11. The disadvantages of black products are as follows:

- Stringent and compartmented OPSEC precautions are required to keep the true identity of the source hidden.
- As they seldom use regular communications channels and must copy opponent characteristics, they are difficult to coordinate within the overall psychological objective.
- Their use may be difficult to control because originating agencies are decentralized.
- Stringent security requirements and long-term campaign plans limit flexibility.
- Operations that use them are extremely vulnerable to discovery, manipulation, and elimination (of equipment and personnel) when operating within opponent territory.
- Operations require stringent oversight procedures and extensive planning that generally preclude timely use below the strategic level.

Appendix B

PSYOP SUPPORT TO INTERNMENT/RESETTLEMENT OPERATIONS

I/R PROGRAMS

B-1. Under U.S. national policy and international laws, the USG must care for and safeguard EPWs, CIs, and DCs captured or taken by U.S. troops. The military police (MP) I/R command or brigade evacuates, processes, interns, controls, employs, and releases EPWs, CIs, and DCs within the Army.

B-2. During stability and support IR operations, PSYOP can assist peacetime programs by pretesting and posttesting products to determine their effectiveness within the HN. Also, they can provide demographic profile information to appropriate U.S. agencies, as well as other PSYOP personnel.

B-3. During a conflict, detained persons are continuous sources of current information accessible to the PSYOP community. If under U.S. control, PSYOP elements may use these individuals, with their consent, to pretest and posttest products.

B-4. Tactical POBs support I/R operations while working with MPs at corps-level holding areas. One TPC should be attached to the MP brigade (I/R). This will allow for support of one TPD per battalion (I/R) that is responsible for an I/R camp. The number of TPDs involved will depend upon the number and size of I/R camps. Corps-level holding areas provide the first semipermanent stopping point for detainees after capture. Access to the corps holding areas allows tactical PSYOP elements to use support to the I/R mission in order to provide timely PSYOP-relevant information. The tactical PSYOP detachment in the camp can also pretest PSYOP products. Also, detainees coming into the corps holding areas provide immediate feedback on the effectiveness of current PSYOP programs. This feedback from the corps holding areas, which hold each detainee from 24 to 48 hours, is a highly valuable source for PSYOP-relevant intelligence. The tactical POB under OPCON to the MP I/R command or brigade supports the POTF. The following paragraphs explain the functions of an I/R PSE.

COLLECT PSYOP INFORMATION

B-5. PSYOP personnel obtain information through interviews, interrogations, surveys, and material they get from detainees. They collect this data for use in the PSYOP process and report it to the POTF or PSE. The TPD quickly transmits perishable tactical PSYOP information collected at the I/R facilities to the POTF for distribution to all PSYOP units.

DISSEMINATE REPORTS

B-6. The tactical POB supporting I/R operations distributes recurring reports to the POTF or PSE. These reports contain data on the numbers, nationalities, and ethnic composition of the facility population. These reports let the POTF or PSE determine if there are suitable TAs in the facility population camp they can use to pretest and posttest products.

SCREEN THE I/R FACILITY POPULATION

B-7. PSYOP personnel screen the facility population for suitable interpreters and translators. Willing and capable detainees can provide a variety of language skills to the PSYOP I/R support team and the facility staff.

INTERVIEW AND SURVEY THE FACILITY POPULATION

B-8. PSYOP personnel can interview and survey detainees to assess the effectiveness of ongoing and previous programs. PSYOP personnel try to determine how and to what extent their messages influenced the EPW to surrender and impacted on their morale or combat effectiveness. PSYOP personnel also try to learn the nature, extent, targets, and goals of the enemy's propaganda to raise the troops' morale and influence the civilian populace in the hostile theater. In addition, interviewers try to discover the goals and priority TAs of the enemy's propaganda directed at U.S. and allied military units.

PSYOP SUPPORT TO I/R FACILITIES

B-9. Large detainee EPW populations represent a military-trained and potentially hostile populace located in the rear area. The populace in the custody of a well-trained and armed MP force thus reduces the threat it presents to U.S. combat operations. This MP force can be a strain on already scarce manpower resources.

B-10. The tactical POB has two missions that reduce the need to divert MP assets to increase security in the I/R facility. The battalion—

- Supports the MP force in controlling detainees through the use of PSYOP.
- Exposes detainees to U.S. and allied policy.

B-11. PSYOP personnel also support the MP custodial mission in the facility. Their tasks include—

- Developing and executing supporting PSYOP programs to condition detainees to accept facility authority and regulations during the detainment period.
- Gaining the detainees' cooperation to reduce MP guard needs.
- Identifying malcontents, trained agitators, and political officers within the facility who may try to organize a resistance or create disturbances within the facility.
- Developing and executing indoctrination programs to reduce or remove pro-enemy support for post-detainment.
- Recognizing political activists (EPW and CI).
- Helping the MP facility commander control the I/R populace during emergencies.
- Executing comprehensive information, reorientation, educational, and vocational programs to prepare the detainees for repatriation.

- Advising the MP facility commander on the psychological impact of actions to prevent misunderstandings and disturbances by the detainees. The difference in culture, custom, language, religious practices, and dietary habits can be so great that misunderstandings are not always avoidable. However, investigation and proper handling can minimize misunderstandings.

B-12. The tactical POB also performs additional tasks. To assist in controlling the facility population, POB personnel react by—

- Improving relations with the local populace to reduce the facility's impact on the local populace, thereby reducing any potential negative impact on facility operations.
- Developing and executing PSYOP programs against opponent partisan forces operating in the rear area.

B-13. PSYOP support of such activities must be coordinated with other PSYOP units having direct responsibility for that area. PSYOP units also coordinate with U.S. and allied rear forces operating within the area. The supporting PSYOP unit commander informs the facility commander of ongoing PSYOP activities in the area that could possibly impact on his internment programs.

B-14. The PSYOP support team usually has direct, unescorted access to the I/R compounds and enclosures. Access to small groups or individual detainees is usually limited to MP/military intelligence (MI) escort. Face-to-face PSYOP are continuous to dismiss potentially disruptive rumors and screen detainee complaints.

B-15. PSYOP personnel cannot coerce detainee contribution to PSYOP products (preparing signed statements or making tape recordings). Prisoners may voluntarily cooperate with PSYOP personnel in the development, evaluation, or dissemination of PSYOP messages or products (Army regulation [AR] 190-8, *Enemy Prisoners of War, Retained Personnel, Civilian Internees, and Other Detainees*). This rule is IAW the laws of land warfare derived from customs and treaties including the Geneva Convention of 12 August 1949, paragraph 1, Article 3: The Hague Conventions and AR 190-8.

FM 3-19.40, *Military Police Internment/Resettlement Operations,* and FM 27-10, *The Law of Land Warfare*, contain further information about detainee rights and treatment.

STABILITY AND SUPPORT OPERATIONS

B-16. I/R operations during stability and support operations do not change. Their importance increases in a counterinsurgency operation. Tactical POB personnel contribute information that may refine TAs for PSYOP programs.

During stability and support operations, I/R facility support teams can perform the following tasks:

- Pretest and posttest products on captured insurgents and civilian internees to determine probable success rates in pacifying the HN TA.
- Determine through interview or interrogation the demographic profile of the insurgents. As a minimum, I/R PSYOP personnel obtain information on the following:
    - Race.
    - Sex.
    - Religious affiliation.
    - Political affiliation.
    - Geographic origin.
    - Education levels.
    - Length, depth, and type of involvement.
    - Previous or current occupation.
    - Standard of living and personal finances.
    - Previous military training.
- Determine and evaluate the effectiveness of the level of political and military indoctrination the insurgents have received to date.
- Cooperate with counterintelligence personnel to identify potential interned insurgents to be used as informants. These informants provide information on active insurgents within the HN's population and its field location. In addition, these informants provide information about insurgent activities within the facility for control purposes.

Appendix C

RULES OF ENGAGEMENT

The ROE reflect the requirements placed on the military by the law of war, operational concerns, and political considerations when the situation shifts throughout the full spectrum of conflict. ROE are the primary means by which the commander conveys legal, political, diplomatic, and military guidelines to his forces.

Operational requirements, policy, and law define ROE. ROE always recognize the right of self-defense, the commander's right and obligation to protect assigned personnel, and the national right to defend U.S. forces, allies, and coalition participants against armed attack. Well-defined ROE are enforceable, understandable, tactically sound, and legally sufficient. Furthermore, explicit ROE are responsive to the mission and permit subordinate commanders to exercise initiative when confronted by an opportunity or unforeseen circumstances.

PSYOP SUPPORT TO ROE

C-1. PSYOP often help minimize ROE violations by ensuring that HN civilians are aware of what behaviors are or are not acceptable to U.S./coalition forces. Violations of the ROE can cause the TA to develop animosity and negativity toward U.S. forces. TAs hostile to U.S. forces may attempt to use ROE violations to further their cause. PSYOP Soldiers should be prepared to minimize repercussions through carefully coordinated supporting PSYOP programs. Reinforcing previous accomplishments and assistance provided by U.S. forces are examples of the types of supporting programs that can help sustain a positive attitude of the TAs.

C-2. The type of ROE will depend on the type of mission. During wartime, the ROE are usually lethal in nature. In MOOTW, the ROE are usually nonlethal in nature and should closely resemble the standing rules of engagement (SROE).

WARTIME ROE

C-3. In general, ROE during wartime permit U.S. forces to engage all identified enemy targets, regardless of whether those targets represent an actual or immediate threat. Wartime ROE are familiar to units and Soldiers because battle-focused training concentrates on combat tasks.

MOOTW ROE

C-4. During MOOTW, the SROE merely permit engagement in individual, unit, or national self-defense. The ROE in MOOTW are generally more restrictive, detailed, and sensitive to political concerns than in wartime. Restrained, judicious use of force is necessary; excessive force undermines the legitimacy of the operation and jeopardizes political objectives. MOOTW ROE considerations may include balancing force protection and harm to innocent civilians or nonmilitary areas, balancing mission accomplishment with political considerations, protecting evacuees while not having the authority to preempt hostile actions by proactive military measures, enabling Soldiers to properly balance initiative and restraint, determining the extent to which soldiers may protect HN or third-nation civilians, the use of riot control agents, and the use of PSYOP. In multinational operations, developing ROE acceptable to all troop-contributing nations is important. Responsiveness to changing ROE requirements is also important.

C-5. The principles of necessity and proportionality help define the peacetime justification to use force in self-defense and are thus fundamental to understanding ROE for MOOTW. The principle of necessity permits friendly forces to engage only those forces committing hostile acts or clearly demonstrating hostile intent. This formulation—a restrictive rule for the use of force—captures the essence of peacetime necessity under international law. The rule of necessity applies to individuals as well as to military units or sovereign states. In 1840, Secretary of State Daniel

Webster described the essence of the necessity rule as the use of force in self-defense is justified only in cases in which "the necessity of that self-defense is instant, overwhelming and leaving no choice of means and no moment for deliberation."

- A *hostile act* is an attack or other use of force.
- *Hostile intent* "is the threat of imminent use of force." ROE take into consideration the important distinction between a hostile act and a hostile intent. ROE describe specific behaviors as hostile acts or equate particular objective characteristics with hostile intent. For instance, the ROE might define a foreign uniformed Soldier aiming a machine-gun from behind a prepared firing position as a clear demonstration of hostile intent, regardless of whether that Soldier truly intends to harm U.S. forces.

C-6. The principle of proportionality requires that the force is reasonable in intensity, duration, and magnitude. The type of force should be based on all available facts known to the commander at the time, decisively counter the hostile act or hostile intent, and ensure the continued safety of U.S. forces. As with necessity, the proportionality principle reflects an ancient international legal norm.

PSYCHOLOGICAL IMPACT

C-7. ROE are legal, political, and diplomatic in nature. These fundamental ideas can have a psychological effect when the ROE are observed and when they are not. The PSYOP Soldier needs to fully understand the ROE and the effects the ROE's execution has on the various TAs within the operational area. The PSYOP Soldier should assist the SJA and the commander to develop the ROE by advising them on the psychological impact of certain actions based on culture, traditions, and so on.

C-8. Successful compliance with the ROE by U.S. forces can be used as a basis for furthering acceptance and trust by the TAs. The PSYOP Soldier can emphasize respect for protected sites such as religious shrines, hospitals, and schools. The PSYOP Soldier can also emphasize respect for the TA, their culture, history, and future.

RULES OF INTERACTION

C-9. Rules of interaction (ROI) apply to the human dimension of SOSO. They spell out with whom, under what circumstances, and to what extent Soldiers may interact with other forces and the civilian populace. ROI, when applied with good interpersonal communication (IPC) skills, improve the Soldier's ability to accomplish the mission while reducing possible hostile confrontations. ROI and IPC, by enhancing the Soldier's persuasion, negotiation, and communication skills, also improve his survivability. ROI founded on firm ROE provide the Soldier with the tools to address unconventional threats, such as political friction, ideologies, cultural idiosyncrasies, and religious beliefs and rituals. ROI must be regionally and culturally specific. They lay the foundation for successful relationships with the myriad of factions and individuals that play critical roles in operations. ROI encompass an array of interpersonal communications skills, such as persuasion and negotiation.

C-10. ROI enhance the Soldier's survivability and, therefore, their reinforcement is critical. PSYOP planners contribute to the development of ROI by providing cultural and TA specific expertise. Participation in the ROI development process can mitigate the potential negative impact of Soldiers violating the accepted standards of behavior, dress, or speech in the given AO.

C-11. Restrictions imposed by ROI may have significant impact on PSYOP. ROI may dictate TA or media selection, as well as time and manner of dissemination. Input on the planning of proposed ROI will ensure that restrictions on PSYOP's ability to access TAs is minimized.

Appendix D

DIGITIZATION OF PSYOP ASSETS

COMMAND AND CONTROL

D-1. When fielded, PSYOP forces at all levels use digital tools to exercise C2 of subordinate units. PSYOP forces use Maneuver Control System (MCS) and GCCS to perform the following C2 functions:

- Participate in the MDMP.
- Transmit and receive PSYOP orders, annexes, overlays, FRAGOs, CONPLANs, and other instructions to subordinate and higher units.
- Submit SITREPs to higher PSYOP HQ.
- Coordinate for higher-level PSYOP support—for example, EC-130E/J COMMANDO SOLO.

ARMY BATTLE COMMAND SYSTEM

D-2. The ABCS is the integration of C2 systems at all echelons. The ABCS integrates battlespace automation systems and communications that functionally link installations and mobile networks. The ABCS is interoperable with joint and multinational C2 systems at upper echelons, across the full range of C2 functionality. At the tactical and operational levels, integration is vertical and horizontal. The ABCS consists of three major components:

- Global Command and Control System—Army (GCCS-A).
- Army Tactical Command and Control System.
- Force XXI Battle Command, Brigade and Below (FBCB2).

GLOBAL COMMAND AND CONTROL SYSTEM–ARMY

D-3. The GCCS-A is a system built from application programs of the following systems:

- Army Worldwide Military Command and Control System (WWMCS) Information System (AWIS).
- Strategic Theater Command and Control System (STCCS).
- EAC portion of the Combat Service Support Control System (CSSCS).

D-4. The primary scope of the GCCS-A effort is to evolve the stand-alone systems into a suite of modular applications that operate within the defense information infrastructure (DII) common operating environment (COE). GCCS-A modules interface with common applications and other shared components of the ABCS and with the joint C2 mission applications provided by the GCCS.

D-5. The GCCS-A is the Army link for ABCS to the GCCS. GCCS-A provides information and decision support to Army strategic-, operational-, and theater- level planning and operational or theater operations and sustainment. GCCS-A supports the apportionment, allocation, logistical support, and deployment of Army forces to the combatant commands. Functionality includes force tracking, HN and CAO support, theater air defense, targeting, PSYOP, C2, logistics, medical, provost marshal (PM), CD, and personnel status. GCCS-A is deployed from theater EAC elements to division.

ARMY TACTICAL COMMAND AND CONTROL SYSTEM

D-6. The Army Tactical Command and Control System (ATCCS) consists of five major subsystems. These subsystems are explained in the following paragraphs.

MANEUVER CONTROL SYSTEM

D-7. The MCS is the primary battle command (BC) source. The MCS provides the COP, decision aids, and overlay capabilities to support the tactical commander and the staff through interface with the force-level information database populated from the Battlefield Automated Systems (BASs). The MCS provides the functional common applications necessary to access and manipulate the Joint Common Database (JCDB). The MCS satisfies information requirements for a specific operation. The MCS tracks resources, displays situational awareness, provides timely control of current combat operations (offense, defense, stability, and support), and effectively develops and distributes plans, orders, and estimates in support of future operations. The MCS supports the MDMP and is deployed from corps to the maneuver battalions.

ALL-SOURCE ANALYSIS SYSTEM

D-8. The All-Source Analysis System (ASAS) is the intelligence and electronic warfare (IEW) component from EAC to battalion. The ASAS is a mobile, tactically deployable, computer-assisted IEW processing, analysis, reporting, and technical control system. The ASAS receives and rapidly processes large volumes of combat information and sensor reports from all sources to provide timely and accurate targeting information, intelligence products, and threat alerts. The ASAS consists of evolutionary modules that perform systems operations management, systems security, collection management, intelligence processing and reporting, high-value or high-payoff target processing and nominations, and communications processing and interfacing.

D-9. The ASAS remote workstation (RWS) provides automated support to the doctrinal functions of intelligence staff officers—division or higher G-2 and battalion or brigade S-2—from EAC to battalion, including SOF. The ASAS RWS also operates as the technical control portion of the intelligence node of ABCS to provide current IEW and enemy situation (ENSIT) information to the JCDB for access and use by ABCS users. The ASAS produces the ENSIT portion of the COP of the battlefield disseminated by means of the ABCS network.

COMBAT SERVICE SUPPORT CONTROL SYSTEM

D-10. CSSCS provides critical, timely, integrated, and accurate automated CSS information, including all classes of supplies, field services, maintenance, medical, personnel, and movements to CSS, maneuver and theater commanders, and logistics and special staffs. Critical resource information is drawn from manual resources and the standard Army multicommand management information system (STAMMIS) at each echelon, which evolve to the Global Combat Service Support—Army (GCSS-A) (the unclassified logistics wholesale and resale business end connectivity). The CSSCS processes, analyzes, and integrates resource information to support evaluation of current and projected force-sustainment capabilities. The chaplaincy is an active participant in CSSCS and is included in the development of CSS services. CSSCS provides CSS information for the commanders and staff and is deployed from EAC to battalion.

AIR AND MISSILE DEFENSE PLANNING AND CONTROL SYSTEM

D-11. The Air and Missile Defense Planning and Control System (AMDPCS) integrates air defense fire units, sensors, and C2 centers into a coherent system capable of defeating or denying the aerial threat, such as unmanned aerial vehicles, helicopters, and fixed-wing aircraft. The AMDPCS provides for automated, seamless C2 and Force XXI vertical and horizontal interoperability with joint and coalition forces for United States Army (USA) air and missile defense (AMD) units. The system provides common hardware and software modules, at all echelons of command, which provide for highly effective employment of Army AMD weapon systems as part of the joint force. AMDPCS provides the third dimension situational awareness component of the COP. Initially, the Air and Missile Defense Workstation (AMDWS) provides elements from EAC to battalion the capability to track the air and missile defense battle (force operations [FO]).

ADVANCED FIELD ARTILLERY TACTICAL DATA SYSTEM

D-12. The Advanced Field Artillery Tactical Data System (AFATDS) provides automated decision support for the fire support (FS) functional subsystem, including joint and combined fires—for example, naval gunfire and close air support. AFATDS provides a fully integrated FS C2 system, giving the fire support coordinator (FSCOORD) automated support for planning, coordinating, controlling, and executing close support, counterfire, interdiction, and air defense suppression fires. AFATDS performs all of the FS operational functions, including automated allocation and distribution of fires based on target-value analysis. AFATDS is deployed from EAC to the firing platoons. AFATDS provides the FS overlay information to the ABCS common database. AFATDS interoperates with the USAF theater battle management core system (TBMCS) and the United States Navy (USN) and United States Marine Corps (USMC) JMCIS. AFATDS also interoperates with the FS C2 systems with allied countries, including the United Kingdom, Germany, and France.

FORCE XXI BATTLE COMMAND, BRIGADE AND BELOW

D-13. FBCB2 is a suite of digitally interoperable applications and platform hardware. FBCB2 provides on-the-move, real-time, and near-real-time situational awareness and C2 information to combat, CS, and CSS leaders from brigade to the platform and Soldier levels. FBCB2 is a mission-essential subelement and a key component of the ABCS. FBCB2 feeds the ABCS common database with automated positional friendly information and current tactical battlefield geometry for friendly and known or suspected enemy forces. The goal is to field FBCB2 to the tank and Bradley fighting vehicle and other platforms with a common-look-and-feel screen. Common hardware and software design facilitates training and SOP. When fielded tactical PSYOP units (Active Army and RC) and other ABCSs use the FBCB2 extensively.

OTHER ARMY BATTLE COMMAND SYSTEMS

D-14. PSYOP forces use several other ABCSs. The following paragraphs discuss each of these systems.

WARFIGHTER INFORMATION NETWORK

D-15. The Warfighter Information Network (WIN) is an integrated command, control, communications, and computers (C4) network that consists of commercially based high-technology communications network systems. The WIN enables information dominance by increasing the security, capacity, and velocity (speed of service to the user) of information distribution throughout the battlespace. A common-sense mix of terrestrial and satellite communications is required for a robust ABCS. The WIN supports the warfighter in the 21st century with the means to provide information services from the sustaining base to deployed units worldwide.

WIN-TERRESTRIAL TRANSPORT

D-16. The Warfighter Information Network-Terrestrial Transport (WIN-T) portion of the WIN focuses on the terrestrial (nonsatellite) transmission and networking segment of the WIN. The WIN-T is the backbone infrastructure of the WIN architecture, as well as the LAN in support of the ABCS-capable tactical operations center (TOC). The WIN-T provides simultaneous secure-voice, data, imagery, and video-communications services.

TACTICAL INTERNET

D-17. The tactical Internet (TI) enhances warfighter operations by providing an improved, integrated data communications network for mobile users. The TI passes C4I information, extending tactical automation to the Soldier or weapons platform. The TI focuses on brigade and below to provide the parameters in defining a tactical automated data communications network.

LOGISTICS

D-18. PSYOP personnel use CSSCS to process, analyze, and integrate PSYOP-specific resource information to support current and projected PSYOP force sustainment logistically. Supply personnel use CSSCS to track, monitor, and requisition PSYOP-specific equipment and all classes of supply needed by subordinate PSYOP units. PSYOP personnel also use CSSCS to evacuate and transfer damaged or broken equipment and to receive new or repaired PSYOP-specific items.

ANALYSIS

D-19. PSYOP personnel use the numerous intelligence databases and links within ABCS to access all-source intelligence products and services. The ABCS supplements PSYOP-specific DOD and non-DOD intelligence sources. Intelligence sources available through ABCS enhance the ability of PSYOP forces to—

- Conduct TA analysis.
- Counter hostile propaganda.
- Track impact indicators.
- Support I/R operations.
- Conduct pretesting and posttesting of products.
- Submit and track requests for information (RFIs).
- Provide input to the CCIR.
- Manage frequency deconfliction.

The ASAS provides PSYOP intelligence personnel the tools to perform—

- Systems operations management.
- Systems security.
- Collection management.
- Intelligence processing and reporting.
- High-value and high-payoff PSYOP target processing and nominations.
- Communications processing and interfacing.

D-20. The ASAS provides PSYOP personnel with current IEW and enemy situation by means of the JCDB, allowing PSYOP intelligence personnel to monitor current tactical, operational, and strategic situations. This capability enhances the ability of the G-2 and S-2 to recommend modification or exploitation of existing lines of persuasion, symbols, products, series, supporting programs, or programs.

INFORMATION MANAGEMENT

D-21. PSYOP personnel use the ABCS to conduct information management. Through this process, PSYOP personnel can share PSYOP information with all IO disciplines for the purpose of synchronization, coordination, and deconfliction. Specific information management functions include—

- Posting PSYOP SITREPs, PSYOP-specific intelligence reports, and PSYOP products to files or folders accessible by all ABCS users.
- Managing message traffic.
- Managing OPORDs, OPLANs, FRAGOs, CONPLANS, and branch plans and sequels.
- Managing RFIs, IRs, PIR, CSS requests, and administrative support requests.

PSYOP PRODUCTION SYSTEMS AND EQUIPMENT

D-22. There are many systems that are used in order to produce products. The system that is used is based on the type of product to be produced (audio, visual, or audiovisual). An understanding of the capabilities of each available system is vital to properly plan for and timeline out the production as part of the series execution. The following paragraphs provide a brief description of these pieces of equipment.

DEPLOYABLE AUDIO PRODUCTION SYSTEM

D-23. DAPS enables production of professional-quality audio broadcast spots, programs, or PSYOP messages. The system interfaces with the MOC in garrison. Capabilities include audio recording and playback of compact discs (CDs), cassette tapes, and mini-discs.

DEPLOYABLE VIDEO NONLINEAR EDITING SYSTEM

D-24. The deployable video nonlinear editing (DNLE) system is capable of receiving video inputs via VHS, Beta, or Hi-8 format. Utilizing the Avid MCXpress software, this system is able to produce, edit, and record PSYOP video products to VHS, Beta, or Hi-8 format. Additionally, the Flyaway

Avid is capable of converting video between any of the three standards currently used worldwide: PAL, SECAM, or NTSC.

MEDIA PRODUCTION CENTER

D-25. The MPC is a strategic PSYOP asset with the capability of capturing raw audio, video, and visual materials for use in the production of PSYOP products. This is a nondeployable asset located at Fort Bragg, North Carolina. Deployed PSYOP units are able to transmit and receive products and product information through various reachback systems.

THEATER MEDIA PRODUCTION CENTER

D-26. The TMPC is a transportable modular system with the capability to produce, edit, distribute, and disseminate broadcast-quality audio, visual, audiovisual, and digital multimedia products. It is equipped to directly support a major theater war (MTW), a small-scale contingency (SSC), peacetime PSYOP, and theater engagement strategies in any region of the world.

FLYAWAY BROADCAST SYSTEM

D-27. The FABS is a transportable, modular, interoperable system with the capability to disseminate broadcast-quality audio and audiovisual products. This system is also capable of limited audio and video production, facilitating the PSYOP aims of supported division-level commanders.

PSYOP DISTRIBUTION SYSTEM

D-28. The PSYOP distribution system is a state-of-the art, satellite-based PSYOP distribution system consisting of commercial, off-the-shelf (COTS) and base-band equipment. It provides PSYOP forces the capability to use worldwide secure, fully interoperable, long-haul distribution systems to link all PSYOP planners with review and approval authorities, production facilities, and dissemination elements. PDS has applications across the joint arena and is interoperable with the SOMS-B, USAF 193d SOW (EC-130E/J COMMANDO SOLO), the MOC at Fort Bragg, North Carolina, the U.S. Navy's FIWC, and fly-away packages. The PDS receives and transmits broadcast-quality audio and video between PSYOP production and dissemination sites and to approval authorities as required. The PDS is compatible with commercial broadcasting standards. The PDS provides the units the capability to develop, gain approval for, and distribute PSYOP products rapidly and efficiently in support of a theater combatant commander, CJTF, or land component commander. It also provides the capability to network PSYOP news-gathering, development, design, production, distribution, and dissemination assets from the tactical PSYOP company level through the operational or JTF level (JPOTF). PDS links key decision makers and approval authorities to enable the delivery of timely, appropriate, and consistent PSYOP products to selected TAs using a variety of media.

PSYOP PRODUCT DISTRIBUTION SYSTEMS AND EQUIPMENT

D-29. These systems serve to distribute PSYOP products to deployed PSYOP forces worldwide via satellite and digital communications:

- Product Distribution Facility.
- INMARSAT-B.
- SIPRNET/NIPRNET.
- Improved Special Operations Communications Assemblage (ISOCA) Kit.
- TACSAT Communications.

PRODUCT DISTRIBUTION FACILITY

D-30. The PDF is a facility dedicated to house product distribution hardware that enables PSYOP units to distribute products throughout the world via SIPRNET.

INMARSAT-B EARTH STATION

D-31. The INMARSAT-B is a transportable commercial communication terminal used to transmit secure voice and data. It has a self-contained antenna and is secure telephone unit III (STU-III) and facsimile (FAX) supportable.

SIPRNET/NIPRNET

D-32. The SIPRNET/NIPRNET is a commercial off-the-shelf Microsoft Windows-compatible computer system with network adapter. It is used for secure/nonsecure research and distribution.

IMPROVED SPECIAL OPERATIONS COMMUNICATIONS ASSEMBLAGE

D-33. The ISOCA is an assemblage of deployable communications equipment. It includes INMARSAT-B, AN/PSC-5 radio, AN/PRC-150 high frequency (HF) radio, scanner, computer, printer, and video camera. It is used as the communications center in a base station configuration and is secure telephone equipment (STE) compatible.

TACTICAL SATELLITE COMMUNICATIONS

D-34. TACSAT provides PSYOP forces with compact, lightweight, secure, deployable tactical communications. TACSAT is used in either a base station configuration or man-packed for voice, cipher, data, and beacon (LST-5C only). TACSAT models include LST-5C, AN/PSC-5, AN/URC-110, and MST-20.

PSYOP PRODUCT DISSEMINATION SYSTEMS AND EQUIPMENT

D-35. These systems are PSYOP dissemination platforms. They are used to disseminate PSYOP products to TAs within an AOR or JOA:

- SOMS-B.
- Portable AM transmitter, 400 watt (PAMT-400).
- Transportable AM transmitter, 10 kW (TAMT-10).
- Transportable AM transmitter 50 kW (AN/TRQ-44).
- Portable frequency modulation (FM) transmitter, 1000 watt (PFMT-1000).
- Portable FM transmitter, 2000 watt (PFMT-2000).
- Transportable TV transmitter, 5 kW (AN/TSQ 171).

SPECIAL OPERATIONS MEDIA SYSTEMS-B

D-36. The SOMS-B is a PSYOP system consisting of the mobile radio broadcast system (MRBS) and the mobile television broadcast system (MTBS). The SOMS-B has both analog-to-digital audio and video conversion capability, and both the MTBS and the MRBS can be deployed separately. The SOMS-B is capable of producing high-quality audio and video products for PSYOP requirements, and then disseminating those products on commercial AM, FM, and SW frequencies, and on commercial television channels using PAL, SECAM, or NTSC standards. Extremely short range when employed in the tactical environment; therefore, the SOMS-B is most useful as a production studio.

PAMT-400

D-37. The PAMT-400 is a 100–400 watt commercial band medium-wave amplitude-modulated (MW-AM) broadcast system with limited audio production capabilities. The transmitter and antenna can be retuned to a different frequency in 30 minutes. The system can broadcast prerecorded tapes, CDs, mini-discs, and live talent, or be used as a retransmission station.

TAMT-10

D-38. The TAMT-10 is a transportable commercial AM transmitter system. The system also includes limited audio production capabilities. The transmitter can be retuned to a different frequency in 3 hours. The TAMT-10 broadcasts prerecorded tapes (reel, cassette, or cartridge), and live talent, or can be used as a retransmission station.

AN/TRQ-44

D-39. The AN/TRQ-44 is a transportable commercial AM transmitter. The system also includes limited audio production. The AN/TRQ-44 broadcasts prerecorded tapes (reel or cartridge), and live talent, or can be used as a retransmission station.

PFMT-1000 AND PFMT 2000

D-40. The PFMT-1000 and PFMT 2000 are flyaway commercial FM transmitters with limited audio production capabilities. The PFMT-1000/2000 can broadcast prerecorded cassette tapes, compact discs, mini-discs, and live talent. The main difference between the PFMT-1000 and the PFMT 2000 is that the PFMT-2000 has 2000 watts of power, conforming to European specifications.

GLOSSARY

A	airborne
ABCS	Army Battlefield Control System
AC	alternating current (NOTE: Obsolete term for Active Component. The new term is Active Army.)
ACC	air component commander
ADCON	administrative control
adversary	Anyone who contends with, opposes, or acts against one's interest. An adversary is not necessarily an enemy.
ADVON	advanced echelon
AEF	American Expeditionary Force
AFATDS	Advanced Field Artillery Tactical Data System
AFB	Air Force Base
AFIWC	Air Force Information Warfare Center
AFSOC	Air Force special operations component
AIA	Air Intelligence Agency
AM	amplitude modulation
AMD	air and missile defense
AMDPCS	Air and Missile Defense Planning and Control System

AMDWS	Air and Missile Defense Workstation
AO	area of operations
AOR	**area of responsibility**—The geographical area associated with a combatant command within which a combatant commander has authority to plan and conduct operations. (JP 1-02)
AR	Army regulation
ARSOF	Army special operations forces
ARSOLL	Automated Repository for Special Operations Lessons Learned
ARTEP	Army Training and Evaluation Program
ASAS	All-Source Analysis System
ASCC	Army service component commands
ASD(SO/LIC)	Assistant Secretary of Defense (Special Operations and Low Intensity Conflict)
ASG	area support group
ASOC	air support operations center
asset (intelligence)	Any resource—person, group, relationship, instrument, installation, or supply—at the disposition of an intelligence organization for use in an operational or support role. Often used with a qualifying term such as agent asset or propaganda asset. (JP 1-02)
assign	To detail individuals to specific duties or functions where such duties or functions are primary and/or relatively permanent. (JP 1-02)
ASP	ammunition supply point
ATCCS	Army Tactical Command and Control System
ATO	air tasking order

attach	The detailing of individuals to specific functions where such functions are secondary or relatively temporary, e.g., attached for quarters and rations; attached for flying duty. (JP 1-02)
AUTODIN	automatic digital network
auxiliary	In unconventional warfare, that element of the resistance force established to provide the organized civilian support of the resistance movement. (AR 310-24)
Avid	Trade name of a specific commercial editing system used for nonlinear digital editing of audiovisual productions.
AVU	audiovisual unit
AWIS	Army WWMCS Information System
BAS	Battlefield Automated System
BC	battle command
BC2A	Bosnia command and control augmentation
BDA	**battle damage assessment**—The timely and accurate estimate of damage resulting from the application of military force, either lethal or non-lethal, against a predetermined objective. Battle damage assessment can be applied to the employment of all types of weapon systems (air, ground, naval, and special forces weapon systems) throughout the range of military operations. Battle damage assessment is primarily an intelligence responsibility with required inputs and coordination from the operators. Battle damage assessment is composed of physical damage assessment, functional damage assessment, and target system assessment. (JP 1-02)

Beta	Trade name for a commercial videotape format using half-inch-wide videotape housed in a cassette, normally used for recording and mastering digital/analog productions.
bn	battalion
BOS	base operating support
C2	command and control
C4	command, control, communications, and computers
C4I	command, control, communications, computers, and intelligence
CA	**Civil Affairs**—Designated Active and Reserve component forces and units organized, trained, and equipped specifically to conduct civil affairs activities and to support civil-military operations. (JP 1-02)
campaign	A series of related military operations aimed at accomplishing a strategic or operational objective within a given time and space. (JP 1-02)
campaign plan	A plan for a series of related military operations aimed at accomplishing a strategic or operational objective within a given time and space. (JP 1-02)
CAO	Civil Affairs operations
CAP	crisis action planning
CAT	crisis action team
CCIR	commander's critical information requirements
CD	counterdrug; compact disc
CDR	commander

CDRUSSOCOM	Commander, United States Special Operations Command
chain of command	The succession of commanding officers from a superior to a subordinate through which command is exercised. Also called command channel. (JP 1-02)
CI	civilian internee; counterintelligence
CIA	Central Intelligence Agency
Civil Affairs activities	Activities performed or supported by civil affairs that (1) enhance the relationship between military forces and civil authorities in areas where military forces are present; and (2) involve application of civil affairs functional specialty skills, in areas normally the responsibility of civil government, to enhance conduct of civil-military operations. (JP 1-02)
CJ3	combined J-3
CJCS	Chairman of the Joint Chiefs of Staff
CJICTF	Combined Joint Information Campaign Task Force
CJIICTF	Combined Joint IFOR Information Campaign Task Force
CJPOTF	combined joint Psychological Operations task force
CJTF	commander, joint task force
CMEC	Captured Material Exploitation Center
CMO	civil-military operations
COA	course of action
coalition	An ad hoc arrangement between two or more nations for common action. (JP 1-02)

COCOM	combatant command (command authority)
COE	common operating environment
COLISEUM	Community On-Line Intelligence System for End-Users and Managers
combatant command	A unified or specified command with a broad continuing mission under a single commander established and so designated by the President, through the Secretary of Defense and with the advice and assistance of the Chairman of the Joint Chiefs of Staff. Combatant commands typically have geographic or functional responsibilities. (JP 1-02)
COMMZ	communications zone
conditions	Those external elements that affect a target audience over which they have little or no control. Contains three parts: stimulus, orientation, and behavior.
CONOPS	concept of operations
CONPLAN	**concept plan**—operation plan in concept format
contingency	An emergency involving military forces caused by natural disasters, terrorists, subversives, or by required military operations. Due to the uncertainty of the situation, contingencies require plans, rapid response, and special procedures to ensure the safety and readiness of personnel, installations, and equipment. (JP 1-02)
CONUS	continental United States
conventional forces	Those forces capable of conducting operations using nonnuclear weapons. (JP 1-02)
coord	coordination

COP	common operational picture
COS	chief of staff
COTS	commercial, off-the-shelf
counterinsurgency	Those military, paramilitary, political, economic, psychological, and civic actions taken by a government to defeat insurgency. (JP 1-02)
counterpropaganda	Actions or inactions taken to mitigate the effects of propaganda.
crisis	An incident or situation involving a threat to the United States, its territories, citizens, military forces, possessions, or vital interests that develops rapidly and creates a condition of such diplomatic, economic, political, or military importance that commitment of U.S. military forces and resources is contemplated in order to achieve national objectives. (JP 1-02)
critical information	Specific facts about friendly intentions, capabilities, and activities vitally needed by adversaries for them to plan and act effectively so as to guarantee failure or unacceptable consequences for friendly mission accomplishment.
CS	combat support
CSE	communications support element
CSM	command sergeant major
CSS	combat service support
CSSCS	Combat Service Support Control System
CT	counterterrorism
DAO	defense attaché officer

DAPS	Deployable Audio Production System
data	Representation of facts, concepts, or instructions in a formalized manner suitable for communication, interpretation, or processing by humans or by automatic means. Any representations such as characters or analog quantities to which meaning is or might be assigned.
DC	dislocated civilian
DCM	deputy chief of mission
DCO	deputy commanding officer
DCO/RACA	deputy commanding officer/research, analysis, and civilian affairs
DCS	Deputy Chief of Staff
DCSLOG	Deputy Chief of Staff for Logistics
DCSOPS	Deputy Chief of Staff for Operations and Plans
DEA	Drug Enforcement Agency
deception	Those measures designed to mislead the enemy by manipulation, distortion, or falsification of evidence to induce the enemy to react in a manner prejudicial to the enemy's interests.
DIA	Defense Intelligence Agency
DII	defense information infrastructure
DIME	diplomatic, informational, military, and economic
DISN	Defense Information Systems Network
dissem	**dissemination**—The delivery of PSYOP series directly to the TA.

distribution	The movement of completed products from the production source to the point of dissemination. This task may include the temporary physical or electronic storage of PSYOP products at intermediate locations.
diversion	The act of drawing the attention and forces of an enemy from the point of the principal operation; an attack, alarm, or feint that diverts attention. (JP 1-02)
DNLE	Deployable Video Nonlinear Editing system
DLA	Defense Logistics Agency
DOD	Department of Defense
DODAAC	Department of Defense activity address code
DODIPP	Department of Defense Intelligence Production Program
DOS	Department of State
DPPC	Deployable Print Production Center
DS	direct support
DSN	Defense Switched Network
DSU	direct support unit
ENSIT	enemy situation
EPW	enemy prisoner of war
EW	electronic warfare
executive order	Order issued by the President by virtue of the authority vested in him by the Constitution or by an act of Congress. It has the force of law. (AR 310-25)
FABS	flyaway broadcast system

FAX	facsimile
FBCB2	Force XXI Battle Command, Brigade and Below
FBIS	Foreign Broadcast Information Service
FID	**foreign internal defense**—Participation by civilian and military agencies of a government in any of the action programs taken by another government to free and protect its society from subversion, lawlessness, and insurgency. (JP 1-02)
FIWC	fleet information warfare center
FM	field manual; frequency modulation
FNS	foreign nation support
FO	force operations
FOB	forward operational base
force multiplier	A capability that, when added to and employed by a combat force, significantly increases the combat potential of that force and thus enhances the probability of successful mission accomplishment. (JP 1-02)
FP	**force protection**—Security program designed to protect Service members, civilian employees, family members, facilities, and equipment, in all locations and situations, accomplished through planned and integrated application of combatting terrorism, physical security, operations security, and personal protective services, and supported by intelligence, counterintelligence, and other security programs. (JP 1-02)
FRAGO	fragmentary order

FS	fire support
FSCOORD	fire support coordinator
FST	field support team
functional component command	A command normally, but not necessarily, composed of forces of two or more military departments that may be established across the range of military operations to perform particular operational missions that may be of short duration or may extend over a period of time. (JP 1-02)
G-1	Deputy Chief of Staff for Manpower or Personnel
G-2	Deputy Chief of Staff for Intelligence
G-3	Deputy Chief of Staff for Operations and Plans
G-4	Deputy Chief of Staff for Logistics
G-6	Chief Information Officer/Director, Information Systems for Command, Control, Communications, and Computers
G-7	Deputy Chief of Staff for Information Operations
GCC	geographic combatant commander
GCCS	Global Command and Control System
GCCS-A	Global Command and Control System—Army
GCSS-A	Global Combat Support System—Army
GENSER	general service
GI&S	geospatial information and services
GRIS	Global Reconnaissance Information System
GS	general support

GSORT	Global Status of Resources and Training
HA	humanitarian assistance
HF	high frequency
HFAC	Human Factors Analysis Center
HHC	headquarters and headquarters company
HMA	humanitarian mine action
HN	**host nation**—A nation that receives the forces and/or supplies of allied nations, coalition partners, and/or NATO organizations to be located on, to operate in, or to transit through its territory. (JP 1-02)
HNS	host-nation support
HQ	headquarters
HSC	headquarters and support company
HUMINT	**human intelligence**—A category of intelligence derived from information collected and provided by human sources. (JP 1-02)
IAW	in accordance with
IDAD	internal defense and development
IDC	Information Dominance Center
IEW	intelligence and electronic warfare
IFOR	Implementation Force
IIP	international information programs
IMI	international military information
IMINT	imagery intelligence
IMPACTS	information warfare mission planning, analysis, and command and control targeting system

info	information
INFOSYS	information systems
INMARSAT-B	international maritime satellite-B
insurgency	An organized movement aimed at the overthrow of a constituted government through use of subversion and armed conflict. (JP 1-02)
INTELINK	intelligence link
IO	information operations
IOC	information operations cell
IPB	intelligence preparation of the battlespace
IPC	interpersonal communications
IPI	international public information
IPIC	International Public Information Committee
I/R	internment/resettlement
IR	information requirement
ISB	intermediate staging base
ISOCA	Improved Special Operations Communications Assemblage
ISR	intelligence, surveillance, and reconnaissance
IW	information warfare
J-1	Manpower and Personnel Directorate
J-2	Intelligence Directorate
J-3	Operations Directorate
J-4	Logistics Directorate
J-6	Command, Control, Communications, and Computer Systems Directorate

JAG	Judge Advocate General
JCCC	Joint Combat Camera Center
JCDB	Joint Common Database
JCET	joint combined exercise for training
JCMA	Joint Communications Security Monitor Activity
JCMOTF	Joint Civil-Military Operations Task Force
JCS	Joint Chiefs of Staff
JCSE	Joint Communications Support Element
JDISS	Joint Deployable Intelligence Support System
JFACC	joint force air component commander
JFC	joint force commander
JFCOM	Joint Forces Command
JFLCC	Joint Force Land Component Commander
JFMCC	Joint Force Maritime Component Commander
JFSOCC	Joint Force Special Operations Component Commander
JIC	Joint Intelligence Center
JIOC	Joint Information Operations Center
JIPTL	joint integrated prioritized target list
JMCIS	joint maritime command information system
JOA	joint operations area
joint	Connotes activities, operations, organizations, etc., in which elements of two or more military departments participate. (JP 1-02)
joint doctrine	Fundamental principles that guide the employment of forces of two or more military departments in coordinated action toward a

	common objective. It is authoritative; as such, joint doctrine will be followed except when, in the judgment of the commander, exceptional circumstances dictate otherwise. It will be promulgated by or for the Chairman of the Joint Chiefs of Staff, in coordination with the combatant commands and Services. (JP 1-02)
joint force	A general term applied to a force composed of significant elements, assigned or attached, of two or more military departments operating under a single joint force commander. (JP 1-02)
joint operations	A general term to describe military actions conducted by joint forces or by Service forces in relationships (e.g., support, coordinating authority) which, of themselves, do not create joint forces. (JP 1-02)
JOPES	Joint Operation Planning and Execution System
JP	joint publication
JPEC	joint planning and execution community
JPOSTC	Joint Program Office for Special Technical Countermeasures
JPOTF	**joint Psychological Operations task force**— A joint special operations task force composed of headquarters and operational assets. It assists the joint force commander in developing strategic, operational, and tactical psychological operation plans for a theater campaign or other operations. Mission requirements will determine its composition and assigned or attached units to support the joint task force commander. Also called JPOTF. (JP 1-02)
JRFL	Joint Restricted Frequency List

JSC	Joint Spectrum Center
JSCP	Joint Strategic Capabilities Plan
JSOA	Joint Special Operations Area
JSOACC	joint special operations air component commander
JSOC	joint special operations command
JSOTF	joint special operations task force
JTF	**joint task force**—A joint force that is constituted and so designated by the Secretary of Defense, a combatant commander, a subunified commander, or an existing joint task force commander. (JP 1-02)
JULLS	Joint Universal Lessons Learned System
JUSPAO	Joint United States Public Affairs Office
JWAC	Joint Warfare Analysis Center
JWICS	Joint Worldwide Intelligence Communications System
KFOR	Kosovo Peacekeeping Operation
kW	kilowatt
L	land
LAN	local area network
LANTCOM	Atlantic Command
line of persuasion	An argument used to obtain a desired behavior or attitude from the TA. Contains four parts: main argument, supporting arguments, appeal, and technique.
LIWA	Land Information Warfare Activity
LNO	liaison officer

MACOM	major Army command
MASINT	measurement and signature intelligence
MCS	Maneuver Control System
MDCI	multidiscipline counterintelligence
MDMP	military decision-making process
MEB	Marine expeditionary brigade
MEDCOM	U.S. Army Medical Command
media	Transmitters of information and psychological operations products.
MEDLOG	medical logistics
MEF	Marine expeditionary force
METT-TC	mission, enemy, terrain and weather, troops and support available, time available, civil considerations
MEU	Marine expeditionary unit
MFP 11	Major Force Program 11
MI	military intelligence
MIO	maritime interdiction operations
MOA	memorandum of agreement
MOC	media operations complex
MOE	**measure of effectiveness**—Tools used to measure results achieved in the overall mission and execution of assigned tasks. Measures of effectiveness are a prerequisite to the performance of combat assessment. Also called MOE. (JP 1-02)
MOOTW	military operations other than war

MOS	military occupational specialty
MP	military police
MPC	Media Production Center
MPEG	Motion Pictures Expert Group
MRBS	mobile radio broadcast system
MSPD	military support to public diplomacy—Those activities and measures taken by the DOD components to support and facilitate public diplomacy.
MTBS	mobile television broadcast system
MTT	mobile training team
MTW	major theater war
multinational joint Psychological Operations task force	A task force composed of PSYOP units from one or more foreign countries formed to carry out a specific PSYOP mission or prosecute PSYOP in support of a theater campaign or other operation. The multinational joint POTF may have conventional non-PSYOP units assigned or attached to support the conduct of specific missions.
multinational operations	A collective term to describe military actions conducted by forces of two or more nations, usually undertaken within the structure of a coalition or alliance. (JP 1-02)
MW-AM	medium-wave amplitude-modulated
national objectives	The aims, derived from national goals and interests, toward which a national policy or strategy is directed and efforts and resources of the nation are applied. (JP 1-02)
NATO	North Atlantic Treaty Organization

NAVSPECWARCOM	Naval Special Warfare Command
NAWCAD	Naval Air Warfare Center
NBC	nuclear, biological, and chemical
NC	North Carolina
NCO	noncommissioned officer
NEO	noncombatant evacuation operation
NGIC	National Ground Intelligence Center
NGO	**nongovernmental organization**—Transnational organizations of private citizens that maintain a consultative status with the Economic and Social Council of the United Nations. Nongovernmental organizations may be professional associations, foundations, multinational businesses, or simply groups with a common interest in humanitarian assistance activities (development and relief). "Nongovernmental organizations" is a term normally used by non-United States organizations. (JP 1-02)
NIMA	National Imagery and Mapping Agency
NIPRNET	Nonsecure Internet Protocol Router Network
NIWA	naval information warfare agency
NLT	no later than
NMC	nonmission capable
NMJIC	National Military Joint Intelligence Center
NMS	national military strategy
NSA	National Security Agency
NSC	National Security Council

NSDD	National Security Decision Directive
NSN	National Stock Number
NSS	national security strategy
NTSC	A type of video output, established by the National Television Standards Committee of America, in which picture information is delivered as a single electronic signal. (NOTE: NTSC and PAL are not compatible or interchangeable.)
OB	order of battle
OCONUS	outside the continental United States
OGA	other government agency
OIF	Operation IRAQI FREEDOM
OPCON	**operational control**—Transferable command authority that may be exercised by commanders at any echelon at or below the level of combatant command. Operational control is inherent in combatant command (command authority). Operational control may be delegated and is the authority to perform those functions of command over subordinate forces involving organizing and employing commands and forces, assigning tasks, designating objectives, and giving authoritative direction necessary to accomplish the mission. Operational control includes authoritative direction over all aspects of military operations and joint training necessary to accomplish missions assigned to the command. Operational control should be exercised through the commanders of subordinate organizations.

	Normally this authority is exercised through subordinate joint force commanders and Service and/or functional component commands. Operational control normally provides full authority to organize commands and forces and to employ those forces as the commander in operational control considers necessary to accomplish assigned missions. Operational control does not, in and of itself, include authoritative direction for logistics or matters of administration, discipline, internal organization, or unit training. (JP 1-02)
OPFUND	operational funding
OPLAN	operation plan
OPORD	operation order
opponent	An antagonistic force or organization that counters mission accomplishment by military means.
OPSEC	**operations security**—A process of identifying critical information and subsequently analyzing friendly actions attendant to military operations and other activities to: a. identify those actions that can be observed by adversary intelligence systems; b. determine indicators that hostile intelligence systems might obtain that could be interpreted or pieced together to derive critical information in time to be useful to adversaries; and c. select and execute measures that eliminate or reduce to an acceptable level the vulnerabilities of friendly actions to adversary exploitation. (JP 1-02)
OSINT	open-source intelligence

OSD	Office of the Secretary of Defense
PA	public affairs
PAL	**phase alternating line**—A type of video output used OCONUS, established to meet European television standards, in which picture information is delivered. (NOTE: NTSC and PAL are not compatible or interchangeable.)
PAO	public affairs officer
PAW	product/action work sheet
PDC	**Psychological Operations development center**—The PDC is the central core of a POTF and mainly responsible for conducting the PSYOP process. The PDC consists of a target audience analysis detachment, a plans and programs detachment, a product development detachment, and a test and evaluation detachment.
PDD	Psychological Operations product development detachment; Presidential Decision Directive
PDF	product distribution facility
PDS	product distribution system
peacekeeping	Military operations undertaken with the consent of all major parties to a dispute, designed to monitor and facilitate implementation of an agreement (ceasefire, truce, or other such agreement) and support diplomatic efforts to reach a long-term political settlement. (JP 1-02)
peacemaking	The process of diplomacy, mediation, negotiation, or other forms of peaceful settlements that arranges an end to a dispute and resolves issues that led to it. (JP 1-02)

peace operations	A broad term that encompasses peacekeeping operations and peace enforcement operations conducted in support of diplomatic efforts to establish and maintain peace. (JP 1-02)
PERSCOM	personnel command
PFMT	portable frequency modulation transmitter
PIR	**priority intelligence requirements**—Those intelligence requirements for which a commander has an anticipated and stated priority in the task of planning and decision making. (JP 1-02)
PM	provost marshal
PO	**Psychological Operations objective**—A statement of a measurable response that reflects the desired behavioral change of a selected TAs as a result of PSYOP.
POAS	Psychological Operations automated system
POAT	**Psychological Operations assessment team**—A small, tailored team (approximately 4 to 12 personnel) that consists of PSYOP planners and product distribution/dissemination and logistics specialists. The team is deployed to theater at the request of the combatant commander to assess the situation, develop PSYOP objectives, and recommend the appropriate level of support to accomplish the mission.
POB	Psychological Operations battalion
POC	Psychological Operations company; point of contact
POE	port of embarkation; port of entry

POG	Psychological Operations group
POG(A)	Psychological Operations group (airborne)
POTF	**Psychological Operations task force**—A task force composed of PSYOP units formed to carry out a specific PSYOP or prosecute PSYOP in support of a theater campaign or other operations. The POTF may have conventional non-PSYOP units assigned or attached to support the conduct of specific missions. The POTF commander is usually a JTF component commander.
POW	prisoner of war
PPBS	Planning, Programming, and Budgeting System
PPD	plans and programs detachment
production	The transformation of approved PSYOP product prototypes into various media forms that are compatible with the way foreign populations are accustomed to receiving information.
propaganda	Any form of communication in support of national objectives, designed to influence the opinions, emotions, attitudes, or behavior of any group in order to benefit the sponsor, either directly or indirectly. By policy and practice, ARSOF forces use the term to indicate PSYOP conducted by enemy or hostile forces, elements, or groups against U.S. or coalition forces.
PSC	personnel service company
PSE	**Psychological Operations support element**—A tailored element that can provide limited PSYOP support. PSEs do not contain organic command and control capability; therefore, command relationships must be clearly defined.

	The size, composition and capability of the PSE are determined by the requirements of the supported commander. A PSE is not designed to provide full-spectrum PSYOP capability; reachback is critical for its mission success.
PSS	personnel service support
PSYACT	**Psychological Operations action**—An action conducted by non-PSYOP personnel, that is planned primarily to affect the behavior of a TA.
PSYOP	**Psychological Operations**—Planned operations to convey selected information and indicators to foreign audiences to influence their emotions, motives, objective reasoning, and ultimately the behavior of foreign governments, organizations, groups, and individuals. The purpose of Psychological Operations is to induce or reinforce foreign attitudes and behavior favorable to the originator's objectives. (JP 1-02)
PSYOP-enabling action	Action required of non-PSYOP units or non-DOD agencies in order to facilitate or enable execution of a PSYOP plan developed to support a commander, a JTF, a regional commander, or other non-DOD agency.
PSYOP impact indicators	Observable events or intelligence related to the PSYOP effort that aid in determining the degree to which SPOs are being achieved. All impact indicators are either positive or negative and contain a direct or indirect orientation.
PSYOP OPLAN/ OPORD	**Psychological Operations operation plan/ operation order**— The POTF/PSE OPLAN/ OPORD articulates how the PSYOP objectives are going to be accomplished by all the

	subordinate elements (even those detached from the POTF/PSE and attached to a maneuver unit). The OPLAN/OPORD is more complete than the annex or tab written as part of the supported unit's OPLA/ORPORD. This plan must be centrally controlled and promulgated to all PSYOP units involved in the operation in order to ensure that the plan is being executed at all levels.
PSYOP process	A seven phase process that must be completed to conduct PSYOP. It consists of planning, target audience analysis, series development, product development and design, approval, production, distribution, dissemination, and evaluation.
PSYOP product	Any audio, visual, or audiovisual communication intended to change the behavior of foreign TAs.
PSYOP program	All the supporting PSYOP programs and their subordinate series (PSYOP products and actions) that support the accomplishment of one PSYOP objective.
PSYOP tab/appendix	Consist of PSYOP objectives supporting PSYOP objectives, PTAL, and MOE developed to aid the supported commander with accomplishing his mission.
PTA	potential target audience
PTAL	potential target audience list
public diplomacy	Those overt international public information activities of the United States government designed to promote United States foreign policy objectives by seeking to understand, inform, and influence foreign audiences

	and opinion makers, and by broadening the dialogue between American citizens and institutions and their counterparts abroad.
R&A	research and analysis
RC	Reserve Component
RFI	**request for information**—Any specific time-sensitive ad hoc requirement for intelligence information or products to support an ongoing crisis or operation not necessarily related to standing requirements or scheduled intelligence production. (JP 1-02)
RGR	Ranger
RMO	resource management officer
ROE	rules of engagement
ROI	**rules of interaction**—Articulate with whom, under what circumstances, and to what extent Soldiers may interact with other forces and the civilian populace.
RSC	regional support company
RSOI	reception, staging, onward movement, and integration
RWS	remote workstation
S-1	personnel officer
S-2	intelligence officer
S-3	operations and training officer
S-4	logistics officer
S-5	civil-military operations officer
S-6	signal officer

SACEUR	Supreme Allied Command, Europe
SAO	security assistance office
SATCOM	satellite communications
SCAME	Acronym used to remember the steps in analyzing opponent propaganda. The letters stand for "source, content, audience, media, effects."
SCI	sensitive compartmented information
SCIF	sensitive compartmented information facility
SCW	series concept work sheet
SDW	series dissemination work sheet
SECAM	**Sequential Couleur avec Memoire**—The video and broadcasting standard used in France, eastern Europe, Russia, and most of Asia and Africa. SECAM has the same screen resolution of 625 lines and 50-Hz refresh rate as PAL.
SecDef	Secretary of Defense
SEG	series evaluation grid
SEM	series execution matrix
series	All PSYOP products and actions directed at a single TA in support of a specific SPO.
Service component	A command consisting of the Service component commander and command all those Service forces, such as individuals, units, detachments, organizations, and installations under that command, including the support forces that have been assigned to a combatant command or further assigned to a subordinate unified command or joint task force. (JP 1-02)

SF	Special Forces
SFG	Special Forces group
SFOB	Special Forces operational base
SFOD	Special Forces operational detachment
SFODA	Special Forces operational detachment A
SFOR	Stabilization Force
SIAM	Situational Influence Assessment Model
SIGINT	signals intelligence
SIO	senior intelligence officer
SIPRNET	SECRET Internet Protocol Router Network
SITREP	situation report
SJA	Staff Judge Advocate
SO	special operations
SOAR	special operations aviation regiment
SOC	special operations command
SOCRATES	Special Operations Command Research, Analysis, and Threat Evaluation System
SOF	special operations forces
SOFA	status-of-forces agreement
SO/LIC	special operations and low intensity conflict
SOMS-B	Special Operations Media System-Broadcast
SOP	standing operating procedure
SOR	statement of requirement
SOSB	special operations support battalion
SOSCOM	Special Operations Support Command

SOSO	stability operations and support operations
SOTSE	special operations theater support element
SOW	special operations wing
SOWD	special operations weather detachment
special Psychological Operations assessment	A PSYOP intelligence document that focuses on any of a variety of different subjects pertinent to PSYOP, such as a particular target group, significant social institution, or media analysis. A SPA can serve as an immediate reference for the planning and conduct of PSYOP.
SPO	supporting Psychological Operations objective
SPS	special Psychological Operations study
SROE	standing rules of engagement
SSC	small-scale contingency
SSD	strategic studies detachment
STAMMIS	standard Army multicommand management information system
STCCS	Strategic Theater Command and Control System
STE	secure telephone equipment
STP	Soldier training publication
STU-III	secure telephone unit III
supported commander	The commander having primary responsibility for all aspects of a task assigned by the Joint Strategic Capabilities Plan or other joint operation planning authority. In the context of joint operation planning, this term refers to the commander who prepares operation plans or operation orders in response to requirements of the Chairman of the Joint Chiefs of Staff. (JP 1-02)

supporting commander	A commander who provides augmentation forces or other support to a supported commander or who develops a supporting plan. Includes the designated combatant commands and Defense agencies as appropriate. (JP 1-02)
supporting PSYOP program	All actions and products developed in support of a single supporting objective.
SW	shortwave
symbol	A visual, audio, or audiovisual means, having cultural or contextual significance to the TA, used to convey a line of persuasion.
TA	target audience
TAA	**target audience analysis**—Detailed, systematic examination of PSYOP-relevant information to select TAs that can accomplish a given SPO.
TAAD	target audience analysis detachment
TAAP	target audience analysis process
TAAT	target audience analysis team
TAAW	target audience analysis work sheet
TACON	**tactical control**—Command authority over assigned or attached forces or commands, or military capability or forces made available for tasking, that is limited to the detailed, and usually, local direction and control of movements or maneuvers necessary to accomplish missions or tasks assigned. Tactical control is inherent in operational control. Tactical control may be delegated to, and exercised at any level at or below the level of combatant command. (JP 1-02)
TACSAT	tactical satellite

TAMCA	theater Army movement control agency
TAMMC	theater Army material management command
TARBS	transportable amplitude modulation/frequency modulation radio broadcast system
TASOSC	theater Army special operations support command
TBMCS	theater battle management core system
TECHINT	technical intelligence
TED	testing and evaluation detachment
TEP	theater engagement plan
terrorism	The calculated use of unlawful violence or threat of unlawful violence to inculcate fear; intended to coerce or to intimidate governments or societies in the pursuit of goals that are generally political, religious, or ideological. (JP 1-02)
theme	An overarching subject, topic, or idea. Often comes from policy-makers and establishes the parameters for conducting PSYOP.
threat	The ability of an enemy to limit, neutralize, or destroy the effectiveness of a current or projected mission organization or item of equipment. (TRADOC Regulation 381-1)
TI	tactical Internet
TMO	transportation movement office
TMOC	theater media operations center
TMPC	Theater Media Production Center
TOC	tactical operations center

tactical Psychological Operations battalion	PSYOP unit that normally provides tactical and operational level PSYOP support to an Army corps, a Marine expeditionary unit, or a Navy fleet, although it could also provide support at an Army or equivalent headquarters.
TPC	**tactical Psychological Operations company**—PSYOP unit that normally provides PSYOP support to a division (high intensity conflict) or can support a brigade-sized element (SOSO).
TPD	tactical Psychological Operations detachment
TPDD	tactical Psychological Operations development detachment
TPFDD	time-phased force deployment data
TPT	**tactical Psychological Operations team**—PSYOP unit that normally provides PSYOP support to a battalion (combat operations) or can support a company/SFODA team-sized unit (SOSO).
TSC	tactical support center
TSCP	theater security cooperation plan
TSOC	theater special operations command
TS-SCI	top secret-sensitive compartmented information
TTP	tactics, techniques, and procedures
TV	television
UAV	unmanned aerial vehicle
UBL	unit basic load
UCP	Unified Command Plan

UHF	ultrahigh frequency
UN	United Nations
UNAAF	Unified Action Armed Forces
UNICEF	United Nations Children's Fund
unified command	A command with a broad continuing mission under a single commander and composed of significant assigned components of two or more military departments, that is established and so designated by the President through the Secretary of Defense with the advice and assistance of the Chairman of the Joint Chiefs of Staff. (JP 1-02)
Unified Command Plan	The document, approved by the President, that sets forth basic guidance to all unified combatant commanders; establishes their missions, responsibilities, and force structure; delineates the general geographical area of responsibility for geographic combatant commanders; and specifies functional responsibilities for functional combatant commanders. (JP 1-02)
UNITAF	Unified Task Force
UPI	United Press International
U.S.	United States
USA	United States Army
USACAPOC	United States Army Civil Affairs and Psychological Operations Command
USAF	United States Air Force
USAJFKSWCS	United States Army John F. Kennedy Special Warfare Center and School

USAR	United States Army Reserve
USASFC(A)	United States Army Special Forces Command (Airborne)
USASOC	United States Army Special Operations Command
USC	United States Code
USCENTCOM	United States Central Command
USCINCCENT	Obsolete term for Commander in Chief, United States Central Command (NOTE: Term is now Commander, United States Central Command.)
USG	U.S. Government
USIS	United States Information Service
USMC	United States Marine Corps
USMILGP	United States military group
USN	United States Navy
USSOCOM	United States Special Operations Command
USSTRATCOM	United States Strategic Command
UW	**unconventional warfare**—A broad spectrum of military and paramilitary operations, predominantly conducted through, with, or by indigenous or surrogate forces organized, trained, equipped, supported, and directed in varying degrees by an external source. UW includes, but is not limited to, guerrilla warfare, subversion, sabotage, intelligence activities, and unconventional assisted recovery.
UXO	unexploded ordnance
VHF	very high frequency

VHS	**video home system**—Trade name for a commercial videotape format using half-inch-wide videotape housed in a cassette, normally used for distribution.
WARNO	warning order
WIN	Warfighter Information Network
WIN-T	Warfighter Information Network-Terrestrial Transport
WSADS	wind supported aerial delivery system
WWMCS	Worldwide Military Command and Control System
XO	executive officer

BIBLIOGRAPHY

AR 190-8. *Enemy Prisoners of War, Retained Personnel, Civilian Internees and Other Detainees.* 1 October 1997.

CJCS Instruction 3110.05C. *Joint Psychological Operations Supplement to the Joint Strategic Capabilities Plan FY 2002 (CJCSI 3110.01 Series).* 18 July 2003.

DOD Directive 5111.10. *Assistant Secretary of Defense for Special Operations and Low-Intensity Conflict (ASD[SO/LIC]).* 22 March 1995.

DOD Instruction S-3321-1. (S) *Overt Psychological Operations Conducted by the Military Services in Peacetime and in Contingencies Short of Declared War (U).* 26 July 1984.

FM 3-0. *Operations.* 14 June 2001.

FM 3-05.102. *Army Special Operations Forces Intelligence.* 31 August 2001.

FM 3-05.301. *Psychological Operations Tactics, Techniques, and Procedures.* 31 December 2003.

FM 3-13. *Information Operations: Doctrine, Tactics, Techniques, and Procedures.* 28 November 2003.

FM 3-19.40. *Military Police Internment/Resettlement Operations.* 1 August 2001.

FM 5-0 (FM 101-5). *Army Planning and Orders Production.* 20 January 2005.

FM 27-10. *The Law of Land Warfare.* 18 July 1956, with Change 1, 15 July 1976.

FM 34-1. *Intelligence and Electronic Warfare Operations.* 27 September 1994.

FM 34-2. *Collection Management and Synchronization Planning.* 8 March 1994.

FM 100-7. *Decisive Force: The Army in Theater Operations.* 31 May 1995.

FM 100-25. *Doctrine for Army Special Operations Forces.* 1 August 1999.
JP 0-2. *Unified Action Armed Forces (UNAAF).* 10 July 2001.
JP 1-02. *Department of Defense Dictionary of Military and Associated Terms.* 12 April 2001 (Amended through 30 November 2004).
JP 3-0. *Doctrine for Joint Operations.* 10 September 2001.
JP 3-05. *Doctrine for Joint Special Operations.* 17 April 1998.
JP 3-08. *Interagency Coordination During Joint Operations, Volumes I and II.* 9 October 1996.
JP 3-53. *Doctrine for Joint Psychological Operations.* 5 September 2003.
JP 5-0. *Doctrine for Planning Joint Operations.* 13 April 1995.
JP 5-00.2. *Joint Task Force (JTF) Planning Guidance and Procedures.* 13 January 1999.
NSDD 77. *Management of Public Diplomacy Relative to National Security.* 14 January 1993.
NSDD 130. *U.S. International Information Policy.* 6 March 1984.
PDD 68. *U S. International Public Information (IPI).* 30 April 1999.

INDEX

NOTES

NOTES

NOTES

NOTES

NOTES

NOTES

NOTES

NOTES

NOTES